Reading Schedule

이 책은 총 36,954개의 단어로 구성되어 있습니다.(중복 포함, 1페이지는 대략 150단어)
분당 150단어 읽기는 원어민이 말하는 속도입니다. 먼저 이 기준을 목표로 시작해보세요.

● 1회 읽기

날 짜	/	/	/	/	/
시 간	~	~	~	~	~
페이지	~	~	~	~	~

내용 이해도 ☑ 90%이상 ☑ 70% ☑ 50% ☑ 30%이하

리딩속도 계산   246 ÷ [   ] X 150 = [   ]
　　　　　　전체 페이지　　시간(분)　 1페이지 당 평균 단어수　1분당 읽은 단어수

● 2회 읽기

날 짜	/	/	/	/	/
시 간	~	~	~	~	~
페이지	~	~	~	~	~

내용 이해도 ☑ 90%이상 ☑ 70% ☑ 50% ☑ 30%이하

리딩속도 계산   246 ÷ [   ] X 150 = [   ]
　　　　　　전체 페이지　　시간(분)　 1페이지 당 평균 단어수　1분당 읽은 단어수

● 3회 읽기

날 짜	/	/	/	/	/
시 간	~	~	~	~	~
페이지	~	~	~	~	~

내용 이해도 ☑ 90%이상 ☑ 70% ☑ 50% ☑ 30%이하

리딩속도 계산   246 ÷ [   ] X 150 = [   ]
　　　　　　전체 페이지　　시간(분)　 1페이지 당 평균 단어수　1분당 읽은 단어수

식은 죽 먹기야~

- 전체 평가

    체감 난이도　☑ 상　☑ 상중　☑ 중　☑ 중하　☑ 하

    읽기 만족도　☑ 나는 리딩의 고수!
    　　　　　　☑ 좀 잘했군요~
    　　　　　　☑ 노력하세요.
    　　　　　　☑ 난 머리가 안 좋나봐 -.-;

키다리 아저씨

리딩 속도가 빨라지는 영어책 007

키다리 아저씨
Daddy-Long-Legs

2015년 5월 20일 초판 1쇄 인쇄
2015년 5월 25일 초판 1쇄 발행

지은이 진 웹스터
발행인 손건
편집기획 김상배
마케팅 이언영
디자인 김선옥
제작 최승용
인쇄 선경프린테크

발행처 LanCom 랭컴
주소 서울시 영등포구 영신로 38길 17
등록번호 제 312-2006-00060호
전화 02) 2636-0895
팩스 02) 2636-0896
홈페이지 www.lancom.co.kr

ISBN 978-89-98469-78-8

키다리 아저씨

Daddy-Long-Legs

진 웹스터 지음

LanCom
Language & Communication

✥ 『키다리 아저씨』 줄거리

우울한 수요일

상상력이 풍부한 제르샤 에벗은 존 그리어 고아원에 거액의 기부금을 내는 익명의 평의원에게서 대학 등록금과 생활비를 지원 받게 된다. 제르샤의 "우울한 수요일"이라는 글을 읽고 그녀의 작가적 재능을 발견한 평의원은 그녀의 재능을 키워주기로 마음먹었고, 조건은 단지, 한 달에 한 번 자신에게 편지를 쓰는 것뿐이다.

대학생이 된 제르샤

대학에 간 제르샤는 약속대로 평의원에게 편지를 쓰면서, 그를 "키다리 아저씨"라 부른다. 그에 대해 아는 것이라곤 고아원에서 언뜻 본 뒷모습뿐이었기 때문이다. 편지를 통해 대학생활, 자신에 대해 솔직하게 털어 놓으며, 전화번호부와 묘비에서 따온 이름 대신 "주디"라고 불러 달라 한다. 제르샤는 여름 방학 동안 록 윌로우 농장에서 농장 소유주인 저비스와 친분을 쌓게 된다.

대학2년

제르샤는 여전히 평의원에게 그녀의 생활을 자세히 적어 보낸다. 친구의 집에 초대받아 감격하고, 평의원이 보내준 야회복을 입고 무도회에도 가본다. 여름 방학 때 친

구 어머니의 초대를 받지만, 평의원의 지시로 록 윌로우 농장에서 지내게 된다. 두 달 동안이나 편지를 쓰지 않을 정도로 마음이 상했지만, 워낙 명랑하고 따뜻한 성품의 제르샤는 다시 마음을 풀고 농장에서 즐겁게 지낸다. 제르샤는 첫 번째 소설을 판매하고, 장학금을 받는다.

대학3년

여름 방학 동안 유럽에 보내주겠다는 평의원의 제의를, 제르샤는 과분한 호의라 생각하여 거절한다. 제르샤는 매그놀리아에서 과외를 하고, 애디론댁 산장으로 초대받아 가기도 하며 자신의 뜻대로 여름 방학을 보낸다.

대학4년

4학년이 된 제르샤는 교우회지 편집장이 된다. 제르샤는 출판사로부터 소설에 대한 혹평을 받아 좌절하기도 하지만, 다시 새로운 소설을 쓰기 시작한다. 제르샤는 졸업식에 키다리 아저씨를 초대한다.

졸업

키다리 아저씨는 제르샤의 졸업식에 오지 않고 꽃다발만 보낸다. 제르샤는 소설을 판매하여 번 돈을 키다리 아저씨에게 편지와 함께 부친다. 제르샤는 저비스에게 청혼을 받지만, 고아원 출신인 것이 마음에 걸려 거절한다. 키다리 아저씨가 몸이 아프다는 소식을 듣고 걱정이 태산이 된 제르샤는 떨리는 마음으로 그를 만나러 간다. 키다리 아저씨의 집으로 간 제르샤는 저비스가 그의 후원자임을 확인하고 행복에 젖는다.

CONTENTS

Blue Wednesday
10

The Letters of Miss Jerusha Abbott to
Mr. Daddy-Long-Legs Smith
24

Blue Wednesday

The first Wednesday in every month was a Perfectly Awful Day--a day to be awaited with dread, endured with courage and forgotten with haste. Every floor must be spotless, every chair dustless, and every bed without a wrinkle. Ninety-seven squirming little orphans must be scrubbed and combed and buttoned into freshly starched ginghams; and all ninety-seven reminded of their manners, and told to say, 'Yes, sir,' 'No, sir,' whenever a Trustee spoke.

It was a distressing time; and poor Jerusha Abbott, being the oldest orphan, had to bear the brunt of it. But this particular first Wednesday, like its predecessors, finally dragged itself to a close. Jerusha escaped from the pantry where she had been making sandwiches for the asylum's guests, and turned upstairs to accomplish her regular work. Her special care was room F, where eleven little tots, from four to seven, occupied eleven little cots set in a row. Jerusha assembled her charges, straightened their rumpled frocks, wiped their noses, and started them in an orderly and willing line towards the dining-room to engage themselves for a blessed half hour with bread and milk and prune pudding.

Then she dropped down on the window seat and leaned throbbing temples against the cool glass. She had been on her feet since five that morning, doing everybody's bidding, scolded and hurried by a nervous matron. Mrs. Lippett, behind the scenes, did not always maintain that calm and pompous dignity with which she faced an audience of Trustees and lady visitors. Jerusha gazed out across a broad stretch of frozen lawn, beyond the tall iron paling that marked the confines of the asylum, down undulating ridges sprinkled with country estates, to the spires of the village rising from the midst of bare trees.

The day was ended--quite successfully, so far as she knew. The Trustees and the visiting committee had made their rounds, and read their reports, and drunk their tea, and now were hurrying home to their own cheerful firesides, to forget their bothersome little charges for another month. Jerusha leaned forward watching with curiosity--and a touch of wistfulness--the stream of carriages and automobiles that rolled out of the asylum gates. In imagination she followed first one equipage, then another, to the big houses dotted along the hillside. She pictured herself in a fur coat and a velvet hat trimmed with feathers leaning back in the seat and nonchalantly murmuring 'Home' to the driver. But on the door-sill of her home the picture grew blurred.

Jerusha had an imagination--an imagination, Mrs. Lippett told her, that would get her into trouble if she didn't take care--but keen as it was, it could not carry her beyond the front porch of the houses she would enter. Poor, eager, adventurous little Jerusha, in all her seventeen years, had never stepped inside an ordinary house; she could not picture the daily routine of those other human beings who carried on their lives undiscommoded by orphans.

Je-ru-sha Ab-bott

You are wan-ted

In the of-fice,

And I think you'd

Better hurry up!

Tommy Dillon, who had joined the choir, came singing up the stairs and down the corridor, his chant growing louder as he approached room F. Jerusha wrenched herself from the window and refaced the troubles of life.

'Who wants me?' she cut into Tommy's chant with a note of sharp anxiety.

Mrs. Lippett in the office,

And I think she's mad.

Ah-a-men!

Tommy piously intoned, but his accent was not entirely malicious. Even the most hardened little orphan felt sympathy for an erring sister who was summoned to the office to face an annoyed matron; and Tommy liked Jerusha even if she did sometimes jerk him by the arm and nearly scrub his nose off.

Jerusha went without comment, but with two parallel lines on her brow. What could have gone wrong, she wondered. Were the sandwiches not thin enough? Were there shells in the nut cakes? Had a lady visitor seen the hole in Susie Hawthorn's stocking? Had--O horrors!--one of the cherubic little babes in her own room F 'sauced' a Trustee?

The long lower hall had not been lighted, and as she came downstairs, a last Trustee stood, on the point of departure, in the open door that led to the porte-cochere. Jerusha caught only a fleeting impression of the man--and the impression consisted entirely of tallness. He was waving his arm towards an automobile waiting in the curved drive. As it sprang into motion and approached, head on for an instant, the glaring headlights threw his shadow sharply against the wall inside. The shadow pictured grotesquely elongated legs and arms that ran along the floor and up the wall of the corridor. It looked, for all the world, like a huge, wavering daddy-long-legs.

Jerusha's anxious frown gave place to quick laughter. She was by nature a sunny soul, and had always snatched the tiniest excuse to be amused. If one could derive any sort of entertainment out of the oppressive fact of a Trustee, it was something unexpected to the good. She advanced to the office quite cheered by the tiny episode, and presented a smiling face to Mrs. Lippett. To her surprise the matron was also, if not exactly smiling, at least appreciably affable; she wore an expression almost as pleasant as the one she donned for visitors.

'sit down, Jerusha, I have something to say to you.' Jerusha dropped into the nearest chair and waited with a touch of breathlessness. An automobile flashed past the window; Mrs. Lippett glanced after it.

'did you notice the gentleman who has just gone?'

'I saw his back.'

'He is one of our most affluential Trustees, and has given large sums of money towards the asylum's support. I am not at liberty to mention his name; he expressly stipulated that he was to remain unknown.'

Jerusha's eyes widened slightly; she was not accustomed to being summoned to the office to discuss the eccentricities of Trustees with the matron.

'this gentleman has taken an interest in several of our boys. You remember Charles Benton and Henry Freize? They were both sent through college by Mr.--er--this Trustee, and both have repaid with hard work and success the money that was so generously expended. Other payment the gentleman does not wish. Heretofore his philanthropies have been directed solely towards the boys; I have never been able to interest him in the slightest degree in any of the girls in the institution, no matter how deserving. He does not, I may tell you, care for girls.'

'No, ma'am,' Jerusha murmured, since some reply seemed to be expected at this point.

'to-day at the regular meeting, the question of your future was brought up.'

Mrs. Lippett allowed a moment of silence to fall, then resumed in a slow, placid manner extremely trying to her hearer's suddenly tightened nerves.

'Usually, as you know, the children are not kept after they are sixteen, but an exception was made in your case. You had finished our school at fourteen, and having done so well in your studies--not always, I must say, in your conduct--it was determined to let you go on in the village high school. Now you are finishing that, and of course the asylum cannot be responsible any longer for your support. As it is, you have had two years more than most.'

Mrs. Lippett overlooked the fact that Jerusha had worked hard for her board during those two years, that the convenience of the asylum had come first and her education second; that on days like the present she was kept at home to scrub.

'As I say, the question of your future was

brought up and your record was discussed--thoroughly discussed.'

Mrs. Lippett brought accusing eyes to bear upon the prisoner in the dock, and the prisoner looked guilty because it seemed to be expected--not because she could remember any strikingly black pages in her record.

'Of course the usual disposition of one in your place would be to put you in a position where you could begin to work, but you have done well in school in certain branches; it seems that your work in English has even been brilliant. Miss Pritchard, who is on our visiting committee, is also on the school board; she has been talking with your rhetoric teacher, and made a speech in your favour. She also read aloud an essay that you had written entitled, "Blue Wednesday".'

Jerusha's guilty expression this time was not assumed.

'It seemed to me that you showed little

gratitude in holding up to ridicule the institution that has done so much for you. Had you not managed to be funny I doubt if you would have been forgiven. But fortunately for you, Mr.--, that is, the gentleman who has just gone--appears to have an immoderate sense of humour. On the strength of that impertinent paper, he has offered to send you to college.'

'to college?' Jerusha's eyes grew big. Mrs. Lippett nodded.

'He waited to discuss the terms with me. They are unusual. The gentleman, I may say, is erratic. He believes that you have originality, and he is planning to educate you to become a writer.'

'A writer?' Jerusha's mind was numbed. She could only repeat Mrs. Lippett's words.

'that is his wish. Whether anything will come of it, the future will show. He is giving you a very liberal allowance, almost, for a girl who has never had any experience in taking care of money, too liberal. But he planned the matter in detail, and I did not feel free to make any suggestions. You are to remain here through the summer, and Miss Pritchard has kindly offered to superintend your outfit. Your board and tuition will be paid directly to the college, and you will receive in addition during the four years you are there, an allowance of thirty-five dollars a month. This will enable you to enter on the same standing as the other students. The money will be sent to you by the gentleman's private secretary once a month, and in return, you will write a letter of acknowledgment once a month. That is--you are not to thank him for the money; he doesn't care to have that mentioned, but you are to write a letter telling of the progress in your studies and the details of your daily life. Just such a letter as you would write to your parents if they were living.

'these letters will be addressed to Mr. John Smith and will be sent in care of the secretary.

The gentleman's name is not John Smith, but he prefers to remain unknown. To you he will never be anything but John Smith. His reason in requiring the letters is that he thinks nothing so fosters facility in literary expression as letter-writing. Since you have no family with whom to correspond, he desires you to write in this way; also, he wishes to keep track of your progress. He will never answer your letters, nor in the slightest particular take any notice of them. He detests letter-writing and does not wish you to become a burden. If any point should ever arise where an answer would seem to be imperative--such as in the event of your being expelled, which I trust will not occur--you may correspond with Mr. Griggs, his secretary. These monthly letters are absolutely obligatory on your part; they are the only payment that Mr. Smith requires, so you must be as punctilious in sending them as though it were a bill that you were paying. I hope that they will always be respectful in tone and will reflect credit on your training. You must remember that you are writing to a Trustee of the John Grier Home.'

Jerusha's eyes longingly sought the door. Her head was in a whirl of excitement, and she wished only to escape from Mrs. Lippett's platitudes and think. She rose and took a tentative step backwards. Mrs. Lippett detained her with a gesture; it was an oratorical opportunity not to be slighted.

'I trust that you are properly grateful for this very rare good fortune that has befallen you? Not many girls in your position ever have such an opportunity to rise in the world. You must always remember--'

'I--yes, ma'am, thank you. I think, if that's all, I must go and sew a patch on Freddie Perkins's trousers.'

The door closed behind her, and Mrs. Lippett watched it with dropped jaw, her peroration in mid-air.

The Letters of Miss Jerusha Abbott to Mr. Daddy-Long-Legs Smith

215 FERGUSSEN HALL

24th, September

Dear Kind-Trustee-Who-Sends-Orphans-to-College,

Here I am! I travelled yesterday for four hours in a train. It's a funny sensation, isn't it? I never rode in one before.

College is the biggest, most bewildering place--I get lost whenever I leave my room. I will write you a description later when I'm feeling less muddled; also I will tell you about my lessons. Classes don't begin until Monday morning, and this is Saturday night. But I wanted to write a letter first just to get acquainted.

It seems queer to be writing letters to somebody you don't know. It seems queer for me to be writing letters at all--I've never written more than three or four in my life, so please overlook it if these are not a model kind.

Before leaving yesterday morning, Mrs. Lippett and I had a very serious talk. She told me how to behave all the rest of my life, and especially how to behave towards the kind gentleman who is doing so much for me. I must take care to be Very Respectful.

But how can one be very respectful to a person who wishes to be called John Smith? Why couldn't you have picked out a name with a little personality? I might as well write letters to Dear Hitching-Post or Dear Clothes-Prop.

I have been thinking about you a great deal this summer; having somebody take an interest in me after all these years makes me feel as though I had found a sort of family. It seems as though I belonged to somebody now, and it's a very comfortable sensation. I must say, however, that when I think about you, my imagination has very little to work upon. There are just three things that I know:

I. You are tall.

II. You are rich.

III. You hate girls.

I suppose I might call you Dear Mr. Girl-Hater. Only that's rather insulting to me. Or Dear Mr. Rich-Man, but that's insulting to you, as though money were the only important thing about you. Besides, being rich is such a very external quality. Maybe you won't stay rich all your life; lots of very clever men get smashed up in Wall Street. But at least you will stay tall all your life! So I've decided to call you Dear Daddy-Long-Legs. I hope you won't mind. It's just a private pet name we won't tell Mrs. Lippett.

The ten o'clock bell is going to ring in two

minutes. Our day is divided into sections by bells. We eat and sleep and study by bells. It's very enlivening; I feel like a fire horse all of the time. There it goes! Lights out. Good night.

Observe with what precision I obey rules-- due to my training in the John Grier Home.

Yours most respectfully,

Jerusha Abbott

To Mr. Daddy-Long-Legs Smith

1st October

Dear Daddy-Long-Legs,

I love college and I love you for sending me--I'm very, very happy, and so excited every moment of the time that I can scarcely sleep. You can't imagine how different it is from the John Grier Home. I never dreamed there was such a place in the world. I'm feeling sorry for everybody who isn't a girl and who can't come here; I am sure the college you attended when you were a boy couldn't have been so nice.

My room is up in a tower that used to be the contagious ward before they built the new infirmary. There are three other girls on the same floor of the tower--a Senior who wears spectacles and is always asking us please to be a little more quiet, and two Freshmen named Sallie McBride and Julia Rutledge Pendleton. Sallie has red hair and a turn-up nose and is quite friendly; Julia comes from one of the first families in New York and hasn't noticed me yet. They room together and the Senior and I have singles. Usually Freshmen can't get singles; they are very scarce, but I got one without even asking. I suppose the registrar didn't think it would be right to ask a properly brought-up girl to room with a foundling. You see there are advantages!

My room is on the north-west corner with two windows and a view. After you've lived in a ward for eighteen years with twenty roommates, it is restful to be alone. This is the first chance I've ever had to get acquainted with Jerusha Abbott. I think I'm going to like her.

Do you think you are?

Tuesday

They are organizing the Freshman basketball team and there's just a chance that I shall get in it. I'm little of course, but terribly quick and wiry and tough. While the others are hopping about in the air, I can dodge under their feet and grab the ball. It's loads of fun practising--out in the athletic field in the afternoon with the trees all red and yellow and the air full of the smell of burning leaves, and everybody laughing and shouting. These are the happiest girls I ever saw--and I am the happiest of all!

I meant to write a long letter and tell you all the things I'm learning (Mrs. Lippett said you wanted to know), but 7th hour has just rung, and in ten minutes I'm due at the athletic field in gymnasium clothes. Don't you hope I'll get in the team?

Yours always,

Jerusha Abbott

PS. (9 o'clock.)

Sallie McBride just poked her head in at my door. This is what she said:

'I'm so homesick that I simply can't stand it. Do you feel that way?'

I smiled a little and said no; I thought I could pull through. At least homesickness is one disease that I've escaped! I never heard of anybody being asylum-sick, did you?

10th October

Dear Daddy-Long-Legs,

Did you ever hear of Michael Angelo?

He was a famous artist who lived in Italy in the Middle Ages. Everybody in English Literature seemed to know about him, and the whole class laughed because I thought he was an archangel. He sounds like an archangel, doesn't he? The trouble with college is that you are expected to know such a lot of things you've never learned. It's very embarrassing at times. But now, when the girls talk about things that I never heard of, I just keep still and look them up in the encyclopedia.

I made an awful mistake the first day. Somebody mentioned Maurice Maeterlinck, and I asked if she was a Freshman. That joke has gone all over college. But anyway, I'm just as bright in class as any of the others--and brighter than some of them!

Do you care to know how I've furnished my room? It's a symphony in brown and yellow. The wall was tinted buff, and I've bought yellow denim curtains and cushions and a mahogany desk (second hand for three dollars) and a rattan chair and a brown rug with an ink spot in the middle. I stand the chair over the spot.

The windows are up high; you can't look out from an ordinary seat. But I unscrewed the looking-glass from the back of the bureau, upholstered the top and moved it up against the window. It's just the right height for a window seat. You pull out the drawers like steps and walk up. Very comfortable!

Sallie McBride helped me choose the things at the Senior auction. She has lived in a house all her life and knows about furnishing. You can't imagine what fun it is to shop and pay with a real five-dollar bill and get some change--when you've never had more than a few cents in your life. I assure you, Daddy dear, I do appreciate that allowance.

Sallie is the most entertaining person in the world--and Julia Rutledge Pendleton the least so. It's queer what a mixture the registrar can make in the matter of room-mates. Sallie thinks everything is funny--even flunking--and Julia is bored at everything. She never makes the slightest effort to be amiable. She believes that if you are a Pendleton, that fact alone admits you to heaven without any further examination. Julia and I were born to be enemies.

And now I suppose you've been waiting very impatiently to hear what I am learning?

I. Latin: Second Punic war. Hannibal and his forces pitched camp at Lake Trasimenus last night. They prepared an ambuscade for the Romans, and a battle took place at the fourth watch this morning. Romans in retreat.

II. French: 24 pages of the Three Musketeers and third conjugation, irregular verbs.

III. Geometry: Finished cylinders; now doing cones.

IV. English: Studying exposition. My style improves daily in clearness and brevity.

V. Physiology: Reached the digestive system. Bile and the pancreas next time. Yours, on the way to being educated,

Jerusha Abbott

PS. I hope you never touch alcohol, Daddy? It does dreadful things to your liver.

Wednesday

Dear Daddy-Long-Legs,

I've changed my name.

I'm still 'Jerusha' in the catalogue, but I'm 'Judy' everywhere else. It's really too bad, isn't it, to have to give yourself the only pet name you ever had? I didn't quite make up the Judy though. That's what Freddy Perkins used to call me before he could talk plainly.

I wish Mrs. Lippett would use a little more ingenuity about choosing babies' names. She gets the last names out of the telephone book--you'll find Abbott on the first page--and she picks the Christian names up anywhere; she got Jerusha from a tombstone. I've always hated it; but I rather like Judy. It's such a silly name. It belongs to the kind of girl I'm not--a sweet little blue-eyed thing, petted and spoiled by all the family, who romps her way through life without any cares. Wouldn't it be nice to be like that? Whatever faults I may have, no one can ever accuse me of having been spoiled by my family! But it's great fun to pretend I've been. In the future please always address me as Judy.

Do you want to know something? I have three pairs of kid gloves. I've had kid mittens before from the Christmas tree, but never real kid gloves with five fingers. I take them out and try them on every little while. It's all I can do not to wear them to classes.

(Dinner bell. Goodbye.)

Friday

What do you think, Daddy? The English instructor said that my last paper shows an unusual amount of originality. She did, truly. Those were her words. It doesn't seem possible, does it, considering the eighteen years of training that I've had? The aim of the John Grier Home (as you doubtless know and heartily approve of) is to turn the ninety-seven orphans into ninety-seven twins.

The unusual artistic ability which I exhibit was developed at an early age through drawing chalk pictures of Mrs. Lippett on the woodshed door.

I hope that I don't hurt your feelings when I criticize the home of my youth? But you have the upper hand, you know, for if I become too impertinent, you can always stop payment of your cheques. That isn't a very polite thing to say--but you can't expect me to have any manners; a foundling asylum isn't a young ladies'

finishing school.

You know, Daddy, it isn't the work that is going to be hard in college. It's the play. Half the time I don't know what the girls are talking about; their jokes seem to relate to a past that every one but me has shared. I'm a foreigner in the world and I don't understand the language. It's a miserable feeling. I've had it all my life. At the high school the girls would stand in groups and just look at me. I was queer and different and everybody knew it. I could FEEL 'John Grier Home' written on my face. And then a few charitable ones would make a point of coming up and saying something polite. I HATED EVERY ONE OF THEM--the charitable ones most of all.

Nobody here knows that I was brought up in an asylum. I told Sallie McBride that my mother and father were dead, and that a kind old gentleman was sending me to college which is entirely true so far as it goes. I don't want you to think I am a coward, but I do want to be like the other girls, and that Dreadful Home looming over my childhood is the one great big difference. If I can turn my back on that and shut out the remembrance, I think, I might be just as desirable as any other girl. I don't believe there's any real, underneath difference, do you?

Anyway, Sallie McBride likes me!

Yours ever,

Judy Abbott

(Nee Jerusha.)

Saturday morning

I've just been reading this letter over and it sounds pretty un-cheerful. But can't you guess that I have a special topic due Monday morning and a review in geometry and a very sneezy cold?

Sunday

I forgot to post this yesterday, so I will add

an indignant postscript. We had a bishop this morning, and WHAT DO YOU THINK HE SAID?

'the most beneficent promise made us in the Bible is this, "The poor ye have always with you." They were put here in order to keep us charitable.'

The poor, please observe, being a sort of useful domestic animal. If I hadn't grown into such a perfect lady, I should have gone up after service and told him what I thought.

25th October

Dear Daddy-Long-Legs,

I'm in the basket-ball team and you ought to see the bruise on my left shoulder. It's blue and mahogany with little streaks of orange. Julia Pendleton tried for the team, but she didn't get in. Hooray!

You see what a mean disposition I have.

College gets nicer and nicer. I like the girls

Judy at Basket Ball

and the teachers and the classes and the campus and the things to eat. We have ice-cream twice a week and we never have corn-meal mush.

You only wanted to hear from me once a month, didn't you? And I've been peppering you with letters every few days! But I've been so excited about all these new adventures that I MUST talk to somebody; and you're the only one I know. Please excuse my exuberance; I'll settle pretty soon. If my letters bore you, you can always toss them into the wastebasket. I promise not to write another till the middle of November.

Yours most loquaciously,
Judy Abbott

15th November

Dear Daddy-Long-Legs,

Listen to what I've learned to-day.

The area of the convex surface of the frustum of a regular pyramid is half the product of the sum of the perimeters of its bases by the altitude of either of its trapezoids.

It doesn't sound true, but it is--I can prove it!

You've never heard about my clothes, have you, Daddy? Six dresses, all new and beautiful and bought for me--not handed down from somebody bigger. Perhaps you don't realize what a climax that marks in the career of an orphan? You gave them to me, and I am very, very, VERY much obliged. It's a fine thing to be educated--but nothing compared to the dizzying experience of owning six new dresses. Miss Pritchard, who is on the visiting committee, picked them out--not Mrs. Lippett, thank goodness. I have an evening dress, pink mull over silk (I'm perfectly beautiful in that), and a blue church dress, and a dinner dress of red veiling with Oriental trimming (makes me look like a Gipsy), and another of rose-coloured challis, and a grey street suit, and an every-day dress for classes. That wouldn't be an awfully big wardrobe for Julia Rutledge Pendleton, perhaps, but for Jerusha Abbott--Oh, my!

I suppose you're thinking now what a frivolous, shallow little beast she is, and what a waste of money to educate a girl?

But, Daddy, if you'd been dressed in checked ginghams all your life, you'd appreciate how I feel. And when I started to the high school, I entered upon another period even worse than the checked ginghams.

The poor box.

You can't know how I dreaded appearing in school in those miserable poor-box dresses. I was perfectly sure to be put down in class next to the girl who first owned my dress, and she would whisper and giggle and point it out to the others. The bitterness of wearing your enemies' cast-off clothes eats into your soul. If I wore silk stockings for the rest of my life, I don't believe I could obliterate the scar.

LATEST WAR BULLETIN!

News from the Scene of Action.

At the fourth watch on Thursday the 13th of November, Hannibal routed the advance guard of the Romans and led the Carthaginian forces over the mountains into the plains of Casilinum. A cohort of light armed Numidians engaged the infantry of Quintus Fabius Maximus. Two battles and light skirmishing. Romans repulsed with heavy losses.

I have the honour of being,

Your special correspondent from the front,

J. Abbott

PS. I know I'm not to expect any letters in return, and I've been warned not to bother you with questions, but tell me, Daddy, just this once--are you awfully old or just a little old? And are you perfectly bald or just a little bald? It is very difficult thinking about you in the abstract like a theorem in geometry.

Given a tall rich man who hates girls, but is very generous to one quite impertinent girl, what does he look like?

R.S.V.P.

19th December

Dear Daddy-Long-Legs,

You never answered my question and it was very important.

ARE YOU BALD?

I have it planned exactly what you look like--very satisfactorily--until I reach the top of your head, and then I AM stuck. I can't decide whether you have white hair or black hair or sort of sprinkly grey hair or maybe none at all.

Here is your portrait:

But the problem is, shall I add some hair? Would you like to know what colour your eyes are? They're grey, and your eyebrows stick out like a porch roof (beetling, they're called in novels), and your mouth is a straight line with a tendency to turn down at the corners. Oh, you see, I know! You're a snappy old thing with a temper.

(Chapel bell.)

9.45 p.m.

I have a new unbreakable rule: never, never to study at night no matter how many written reviews are coming in the morning. Instead, I read just plain books--I have to, you know, because there are eighteen blank years behind me. You wouldn't believe, Daddy, what an abyss of ignorance my mind is; I am just realizing the depths myself. The things that most girls with

a properly assorted family and a home and
friends and a library know by absorption, I have
never heard of. For example:

I never read Mother Goose or David Copperfield or Ivanhoe or Cinderella or Blue Beard or Robinson Crusoe or Jane Eyre or Alice in Wonderland or a word of Rudyard Kipling. I didn't know that Henry the Eighth was married more than once or that Shelley was a poet. I didn't know that people used to be monkeys and that the Garden of Eden was a beautiful myth. I didn't know that R. L. S. stood for Robert Louis Stevenson or that George Eliot was a lady. I had never seen a picture of the 'mona Lisa' and (it's true but you won't believe it) I had never heard of Sherlock Holmes.

Now, I know all of these things and a lot of others besides, but you can see how much I need to catch up. And oh, but it's fun! I look forward all day to evening, and then I put an 'engaged' on the door and get into my nice red bath robe and furry slippers and pile all the cushions behind me on the couch, and light the brass student lamp at my elbow, and read and read and read one book isn't enough. I have four going at once. Just now, they're Tennyson's poems and Vanity Fair and Kipling's Plain Tales and--don't laugh--Little Women. I find that I am the only girl in college who wasn't brought up on Little Women. I haven't told anybody though (that WOULD stamp me as queer). I just quietly went and bought it with $1.12 of my last month's allowance; and the next time somebody mentions pickled limes, I'll know what she is talking about!

(Ten o'clock bell. This is a very interrupted letter.)

Saturday

Sir,

I have the honour to report fresh explorations in the field of geometry. On Friday last we

abandoned our former works in parallelopipeds
and proceeded to truncated prisms. We are finding the road rough and very uphill.

Sunday

The Christmas holidays begin next week and the trunks are up. The corridors are so filled up that you can hardly get through, and everybody is so bubbling over with excitement that studying is getting left out. I'm going to have a beautiful time in vacation; there's another Freshman who lives in Texas staying behind, and we are planning to take long walks and if there's any ice--learn to skate. Then there is still the whole library to be read--and three empty weeks to do it in!

Goodbye, Daddy, I hope that you are feeling as happy as am.

Yours ever,

Judy

PS. Don't forget to answer my question. If

you don't want the trouble of writing, have your secretary telegraph. He can just say:

Mr. Smith is quite bald, or Mr. Smith is not bald, or Mr. Smith has white hair.

And you can deduct the twenty-five cents out of my allowance.

Goodbye till January--and a merry Christ-mas!

Towards the end of the Christmas vacation.
Exact date unknown
Dear Daddy-Long-Legs,

Is it snowing where you are? All the world that I see from my tower is draped in white and the flakes are coming down as big as pop-corns. It's late afternoon--the sun is just setting (a cold yellow colour) behind some colder violet hills, and I am up in my window seat using the last light to write to you.

Your five gold pieces were a surprise! I'm not used to receiving Christmas presents. You have already given me such lots of things--everything I have, you know--that I don't quite feel that I deserve extras. But I like them just the same. Do you want to know what I bought with my money?

    I. A silver watch in a leather case to wear on my wrist and get me to recitations in time.

    II. Matthew Arnold's poems.

    III. A hot water bottle.

    IV. A steamer rug. (My tower is cold.)

    V. Five hundred sheets of yellow manuscript paper. (I'm going to commence being an author pretty soon.)

    VI. A dictionary of synonyms. (To enlarge the author's vocabulary.)

    VII. (I don't much like to confess this last item, but I will.) A pair of silk stockings.

And now, Daddy, never say I don't tell all!

It was a very low motive, if you must know it, that prompted the silk stockings. Julia Pendleton comes into my room to do geometry, and she sits cross-legged on the couch and wears silk stockings every night. But just wait--as soon as she gets back from vacation I shall go in and sit on her couch in my silk stockings. You see, Daddy, the miserable creature that I am but at least I'm honest; and you knew already, from my asylum record, that I wasn't perfect, didn't you?

To recapitulate (that's the way the English instructor begins every other sentence), I am very much obliged for my seven presents. I'm pretending to myself that they came in a box from my family in California. The watch is from father, the rug from mother, the hot water bottle from grandmother who is always worrying for fear I shall catch cold in this climate--and the yellow paper from my little brother Harry. My sister Isabel gave me the silk stockings, and Aunt Susan the Matthew Arnold poems; Uncle Harry (little Harry is named after him) gave me the dictionary. He wanted to send chocolates, but I insisted on synonyms.

You don't object, do you, to playing the part of a composite family?

And now, shall I tell you about my vacation, or are you only interested in my education as such? I hope you appreciate the delicate shade of meaning in 'as such'. It is the latest addition to my vocabulary.

The girl from Texas is named Leonora Fenton. (Almost as funny as Jerusha, isn't it?) I like her, but not so much as Sallie McBride; I shall never like any one so much as Sallie-- except you. I must always like you the best of all, because you're my whole family rolled into one. Leonora and I and two Sophomores have walked 'cross country every pleasant day and explored the whole neighbourhood, dressed in short skirts and knit jackets and caps, and carrying shiny sticks to whack things with. Once we walked into town--four miles--and stopped at a restaurant where the college girls go for dinner. Broiled lobster (35 cents), and for dessert, buckwheat cakes and maple syrup (15 cents). Nourishing and cheap.

It was such a lark! Especially for me, because it was so awfully different from the asylum--I feel like an escaped convict every time I leave the campus. Before I thought, I started to tell the others what an experience I was having. The cat was almost out of the bag when I grabbed it by its tail and pulled it back. It's awfully hard for me not to tell everything I know. I'm a very confiding soul by nature; if I didn't have you to tell things to, I'd burst.

We had a molasses candy pull last Friday evening, given by the house matron of Fergussen to the left-behinds in the other halls. There were twenty-two of us altogether, Freshmen and Sophomores and juniors and Seniors all united in amicable accord. The kitchen is huge, with copper pots and kettles hanging in rows on the stone wall--the littlest casserole among them about the size of a wash boiler. Four hundred girls live in Fergussen. The chef, in a white cap and apron, fetched out twenty-two other white caps and aprons--I can't imagine where he got so many--and we all turned ourselves into cooks.

It was great fun, though I have seen better candy. When it was finally finished, and ourselves and the kitchen and the door-knobs all thoroughly sticky, we organized a procession and still in our caps and aprons, each carrying a big fork or spoon or frying pan, we marched through the empty corridors to the officers' parlour, where half-a-dozen professors and instructors were passing a tranquil evening. We serenaded them with college songs and offered refreshments. They accepted politely but dubiously. We left them sucking chunks of molasses candy, sticky and speechless.

So you see, Daddy, my education progresses! Don't you really think that I ought to be an artist instead of an author?

Vacation will be over in two days and I shall be glad to see the girls again. My tower is just a trifle lonely; when nine people occupy a house that was built for four hundred, they do rattle around a bit.

Eleven pages--poor Daddy, you must be tired! I meant this to be just a short little thank-you note--but when I get started I seem to have a ready pen.

Goodbye, and thank you for thinking of me--I should be perfectly happy except for one little threatening cloud on the horizon. Examinations come in February.

Yours with love,

Judy

PS. Maybe it isn't proper to send love? If it isn't, please excuse. But I must love somebody and there's only you and Mrs. Lippett to choose between, so you see--you'll HAVE to put up with it, Daddy dear, because I can't love her.

On the Eve

Dear Daddy-Long-Legs,

You should see the way this college is studying! We've forgotten we ever had a vacation. Fifty-seven irregular verbs have I introduced to my brain in the past four days--I'm only hoping they'll stay till after examinations.

Some of the girls sell their text-books when they're through with them, but I intend to keep mine. Then after I've graduated I shall have my whole education in a row in the bookcase, and when I need to use any detail, I can turn to it without the slightest hesitation. So much easier and more accurate than trying to keep it in your head.

Julia Pendleton dropped in this evening to pay a social call, and stayed a solid hour. She got started on the subject of family, and I COULDN't switch her off. She wanted to know what my mother's maiden name was--did you ever hear such an impertinent question to ask of a person from a foundling asylum? I didn't have the courage to say I didn't know, so I just miserably plumped on the first name I could think of, and that was Montgomery. Then she wanted to know whether I belonged to the Massachusetts Montgomerys or the Virginia Montgomerys.

Her mother was a Rutherford. The family came over in the ark, and were connected by marriage with Henry the VIII. On her father's side they date back further than Adam. On the topmost branches of her family tree there's a superior breed of monkeys with very fine silky hair and extra long tails.

I meant to write you a nice, cheerful, entertaining letter tonight, but I'm too sleepy--and scared. The Freshman's lot is not a happy one.

Yours, about to be examined,

Judy Abbott

Sunday

Dearest Daddy-Long-Legs,

I have some awful, awful, awful news to tell you, but I won't begin with it; I'll try to get you in a good humour first.

Jerusha Abbott has commenced to be an author. A poem entitled, 'From my Tower', appears in the February Monthly--on the first page, which is a very great honour for a Freshman. My English instructor stopped me on the way out from chapel last night, and said it was a

NEWS of the MONTH

Judy learns to skate

And to vault a bar

Also to slide down a rope

Legs are very difficult!

She receives two flunk notes and sheds many tears

But promises to study HARD

charming piece of work except for the sixth line, which had too many feet. I will send you a copy in case you care to read it.

Let me see if I can't think of something else pleasant-- Oh, yes! I'm learning to skate, and can glide about quite respectably all by myself. Also I've learned how to slide down a rope from the roof of the gymnasium, and I can vault a bar three feet and six inches high--I hope shortly to pull up to four feet.

We had a very inspiring sermon this morning preached by the Bishop of Alabama. His text was: 'Judge not that ye be not judged.' It was about the necessity of overlooking mistakes in others, and not discouraging people by harsh judgments. I wish you might have heard it.

This is the sunniest, most blinding winter afternoon, with icicles dripping from the fir trees and all the world bending under a weight of snow--except me, and I'm bending under a weight of sorrow.

Now for the news--courage, Judy!--you must tell.

Are you SURELY in a good humour? I failed in mathematics and Latin prose. I am tutoring in them, and will take another examination next month. I'm sorry if you're disappointed, but otherwise I don't care a bit because I've learned such a lot of things not mentioned in the catalogue. I've read seventeen novels and bushels of poetry--really necessary novels like Vanity Fair and Richard Feverel and Alice in Wonderland. Also Emerson's Essays and Lockhart's Life of Scott and the first volume of Gibbon's Roman Empire and half of Benvenuto Cellini's Life--wasn't he entertaining? He used to saunter out and casually kill a man before breakfast.

So you see, Daddy, I'm much more intelligent than if I'd just stuck to Latin. Will you forgive me this once if I promise never to fail again?

Yours in sackcloth,

Judy

Dear Daddy-Long-Legs,

This is an extra letter in the middle of the month because I'm rather lonely tonight. It's awfully stormy. All the lights are out on the campus, but I drank black coffee and I can't go to sleep.

I had a supper party this evening consisting of Sallie and Julia and Leonora Fenton-- and sardines and toasted muffins and salad and fudge and coffee. Julia said she'd had a good time, but Sallie stayed to help wash the dishes.

I might, very usefully, put some time on Latin tonight but, there's no doubt about it, I'm a very languid Latin scholar. We've finished Livy and De Senectute and are now engaged with De Amicitia (pronounced Damn Icitia).

Should you mind, just for a little while, pretending you are my grandmother? Sallie has one and Julia and Leonora each two, and they were all comparing them tonight. I can't think of anything I'd rather have; it's such a respectable relationship. So, if you really don't object--When I went into town yesterday, I saw the sweetest cap of Cluny lace trimmed with lavender ribbon. I am going to make you a present of it on your eighty-third birthday.

!!!!!!!!!!!!

That's the clock in the chapel tower striking twelve. I believe I am sleepy after all.

Good night, Granny.
I love you dearly.

Judy

The Ides of March

Dear D.-L.-L.,

I am studying Latin prose composition. I have been studying it. I shall be studying it. I shall be about to have been studying it. My re-examination comes the 7th hour next Tuesday, and I am going to pass or BUST. So you may expect to hear from me next, whole and happy and free from conditions, or in fragments.

I will write a respectable letter when it's over. Tonight I have a pressing engagement with the Ablative Absolute.

Yours--in evident haste
J. A.

26th March

Mr. D.-L.-L. Smith,

SIR: You never answer any questions; you never show the slightest interest in anything I do. You are probably the horridest one of all those horrid Trustees, and the reason you are educating me is, not because you care a bit about me, but from a sense of Duty.

I don't know a single thing about you. I don't even know your name. It is very uninspiring writing to a Thing. I haven't a doubt but that you throw my letters into the waste-basket without reading them. Hereafter I shall write only about work.

My re-examinations in Latin and geometry came last week. I passed them both and am now free from conditions.

Yours truly,

Jerusha Abbott

2nd April

Dear Daddy-Long-Legs,

I am a BEAST.

Please forget about that dreadful letter I sent you last week--I was feeling terribly lonely and miserable and sore-throaty the night I wrote. I didn't know it, but I was just sickening for tonsillitis and grippe and lots of things mixed. I'm in the infirmary now, and have been here for six days; this is the first time they would let me sit up and have a pen and paper. The head nurse is very bossy. But I've been thinking about it all the time and I shan't get well until you forgive me.

Here is a picture of the way I look, with a bandage tied around my head in rabbit's ears. Doesn't that arouse your sympathy? I am having sublingual gland swelling. And I've been studying physiology all the year without ever hearing of sublingual glands. How futile a thing is education!

I can't write any more; I get rather shaky when I sit up too long. Please forgive me for being impertinent and ungrateful. I was badly brought up.

Yours with love,

Judy Abbott

THE INFIRMARY

4th April

Dearest Daddy-Long-Legs,

Yesterday evening just towards dark, when I was sitting up in bed looking out at the rain and feeling awfully bored with life in a great institution, the nurse appeared with a long white box addressed to me, and filled with the LOVE-LIEST pink rosebuds. And much nicer still, it contained a card with a very polite message written in a funny little uphill back hand (but one which shows a great deal of character). Thank you, Daddy, a thousand times. Your flowers make the first real, true present I ever received in my life. If you want to know what a baby I am I lay down and cried because I was so happy.

Now that I am sure you read my letters, I'll make them much more interesting, so they'll be worth keeping in a safe with red tape around them--only please take out that dreadful one and burn it up. I'd hate to think that you ever read it over.

Thank you for making a very sick, cross, miserable Freshman cheerful. Probably you have lots of loving family and friends, and you don't know what it feels like to be alone. But I do.

Goodbye--I'll promise never to be horrid

again, because now I know you're a real person; also I'll promise never to bother you with any more questions.

Do you still hate girls?

Yours for ever,

Judy

8th hour, Monday

Dear Daddy-Long-Legs,

I hope you aren't the Trustee who sat on the toad? It went off--I was told--with quite a pop, so probably he was a fatter Trustee.

Do you remember the little dugout places with gratings over them by the laundry windows in the John Grier Home? Every spring when the hoptoad season opened we used to form a collection of toads and keep them in those window holes; and occasionally they would spill over into the laundry, causing a very pleasurable commotion on wash days. We were severely punished for our activities in this direction, but in spite of all discouragement the toads would collect.

And one day--well, I won't bore you with particulars--but somehow, one of the fattest, biggest, JUCIEST toads got into one of those big leather arm chairs in the Trustees' room, and that afternoon at the Trustees' meeting--But I dare say you were there and recall the rest?

Looking back dispassionately after a period of time, I will say that punishment was merited, and--if I remember rightly--adequate.

I don't know why I am in such a reminiscent mood except that spring and the reappearance of toads always awakens the old acquisitive instinct. The only thing that keeps me from starting a collection is the fact that no rule exists against it.

After chapel, Thursday

What do you think is my favourite book? Just now, I mean; I change every three days.

Wuthering Heights. Emily Bronte was quite young when she wrote it, and had never been outside of Haworth churchyard. She had never known any men in her life; how COULD she imagine a man like Heathcliffe?

I couldn't do it, and I'm quite young and never outside the John Grier Asylum--I've had every chance in the world. Sometimes a dreadful fear comes over me that I'm not a genius. Will you be awfully disappointed, Daddy, if I don't turn out to be a great author? In the spring when everything is so beautiful and green and budding, I feel like turning my back on lessons, and running away to play with the weather. There are such lots of adventures out in the fields! It's much more entertaining to live books than to write them.

Ow!!!!!!

That was a shriek which brought Sallie and Julia and (for a disgusted moment) the Senior from across the hall. It was caused by a centipede like this: only worse. Just as I had finished the last sentence and was thinking what to say next--plump!--it fell off the ceiling and landed at my side. I tipped two cups off the tea table in trying to get away. Sallie whacked it with the back of my hair brush--which I shall never be able to use again--and killed the front end, but the rear fifty feet ran under the bureau and escaped.

This dormitory, owing to its age and ivy-covered walls, is full of centipedes. They are dreadful creatures. I'd rather find a tiger under the bed.

Friday, 9.30 p.m.

Such a lot of troubles! I didn't hear the rising bell this morning, then I broke my shoestring while I was hurrying to dress and dropped my collar button down my neck. I was late for breakfast and also for first-hour recitation. I forgot to take any blotting paper and my fountain pen leaked. In trigonometry the Professor and I had a disagreement touching a little matter of logarithms. On looking it up, I find that she was right. We had mutton stew and pie-plant for lunch--hate 'em both; they taste like the asylum. The post brought me nothing but bills (though I must say that I never do get anything else; my family are not the kind that write). In English class this afternoon we had an unexpected written lesson. This was it:

I asked no other thing,

No other was denied.

I offered Being for it;

The mighty merchant smiled.

Brazil? He twirled a button

Without a glance my way:

But, madam, is there nothing else

That we can show today?

That is a poem. I don't know who wrote it or

what it means. It was simply printed out on the blackboard when we arrived and we were ordered to comment upon it. When I read the first verse I thought I had an idea--The Mighty Merchant was a divinity who distributes blessings in return for virtuous deeds--but when I got to the second verse and found him twirling a button, it seemed a blasphemous supposition, and I hastily changed my mind. The rest of the class was in the same predicament; and there we sat for three-quarters of an hour with blank paper and equally blank minds. Getting an education is an awfully wearing process!

But this didn't end the day. There's worse to come.

It rained so we couldn't play golf, but had to go to gymnasium instead. The girl next to me banged my elbow with an Indian club. I got home to find that the box with my new blue spring dress had come, and the skirt was so tight that I couldn't sit down. Friday is sweeping day, and the maid had mixed all the papers on my desk. We had tombstone for dessert (milk and gelatin flavoured with vanilla). We were kept in chapel twenty minutes later than usual to listen to a speech about womanly women. And then--just as I was settling down with a sigh of well-earned relief to The Portrait of a Lady, a girl named Ackerly, a dough-faced, deadly, unintermittently stupid girl, who sits next to me in Latin because her name begins with A (I wish Mrs. Lippett had named me Zabriski), came to ask if Monday's lesson commenced at paragraph 69 or 70, and stayed ONE HOUR. She has just gone.

Did you ever hear of such a discouraging series of events? It isn't the big troubles in life that require character. Anybody can rise to a crisis and face a crushing tragedy with courage, but to meet the petty hazards of the day with a laugh--I really think that requires SPIRIT.

It's the kind of character that I am going to

develop. I am going to pretend that all life is just a game which I must play as skilfully and fairly as I can. If I lose, I am going to shrug my shoulders and laugh--also if I win.

Anyway, I am going to be a sport. You will never hear me complain again, Daddy dear, because Julia wears silk stockings and centipedes drop off the wall.

Answer soon.

Yours ever,

Judy

27th May

Daddy-Long-Legs, Esq.

DEAR SIR: I am in receipt of a letter from Mrs. Lippett. She hopes that I am doing well in deportment and studies. Since I probably have no place to go this summer, she will let me come back to the asylum and work for my board until college opens.

I HATE THE JOHN GRIER HOME.

I'd rather die than go back.

Yours most truthfully,

Jerusha Abbott

Cher Daddy-Jambes-Longes,

Vous etes un brick!

Je suis tres heureuse about the farm, parceque je n'ai jamais been on a farm dans ma vie and I'd hate to retourner chez John Grier, et wash dishes tout l'ete. There would be danger of quelque chose affreuse happening, parceque j'ai perdue ma humilite d'autre fois et j'ai peur that I would just break out quelque jour et smash every cup and saucer dans la maison.

Pardon brievete et paper. Je ne peux pas send des mes nouvelles parceque je suis dans French class et j'ai peur que Monsieur le Professeur is going to call on me tout de suite.

He did!

Au revoir,

je vous aime beaucoup.

Judy

30th May

Dear Daddy-Long-Legs,

Did you ever see this campus? (That is merely a rhetorical question. Don't let it annoy you.) It is a heavenly spot in May. All the shrubs are in blossom and the trees are the loveliest young green--even the old pines look fresh and new. The grass is dotted with yellow dandelions and hundreds of girls in blue and white and pink dresses. Everybody is joyous and carefree, for vacation's coming, and with that to look forward to, examinations don't count.

Isn't that a happy frame of mind to be in? And oh, Daddy! I'm the happiest of all! Because I'm not in the asylum any more; and I'm not anybody's nursemaid or typewriter or bookkeeper (I should have been, you know, except for you).

I'm sorry now for all my past badnesses.

I'm sorry I was ever impertinent to Mrs. Lippett.

I'm sorry I ever slapped Freddie Perkins.

I'm sorry I ever filled the sugar bowl with salt.

I'm sorry I ever made faces behind the Trustees' backs.

I'm going to be good and sweet and kind to everybody because I'm so happy. And this summer I'm going to write and write and write and begin to be a great author. Isn't that an exalted stand to take? Oh, I'm developing a beautiful character! It droops a bit under cold and frost, but it does grow fast when the sun shines.

That's the way with everybody. I don't agree with the theory that adversity and sorrow and disappointment develop moral strength. The happy people are the ones who are bubbling over with kindliness. I have no faith in misanthropes. (Fine word! Just learned it.) You are not a misanthrope are you, Daddy?

I started to tell you about the campus. I wish you'd come for a little visit and let me walk you about and say:

'that is the library. This is the gas plant, Daddy dear. The Gothic building on your left is the gymnasium, and the Tudor Romanesque beside it is the new infirmary.'

Oh, I'm fine at showing people about. I've done it all my life at the asylum, and I've been doing it all day here. I have honestly.

And a Man, too!

That's a great experience. I never talked to a man before (except occasional Trustees, and they don't count). Pardon, Daddy, I don't mean to hurt your feelings when I abuse Trustees. I don't consider that you really belong among them. You just tumbled on to the Board by chance. The Trustee, as such, is fat and pompous and benevolent. He pats one on the head and wears a gold watch chain.

That looks like a June bug, but is meant to

be a portrait of any Trustee except you.

However--to resume:

I have been walking and talking and having tea with a man. And with a very superior man--with Mr. Jervis Pendleton of the House of Julia; her uncle, in short (in long, perhaps I ought to say; he's as tall as you.) Being in town on business, he decided to run out to the college and call on his niece. He's her father's youngest brother, but she doesn't know him very intimately. It seems he glanced at her when she was a baby, decided he didn't like her, and has never noticed her since.

Anyway, there he was, sitting in the reception room very proper with his hat and stick and gloves beside him; and Julia and Sallie with seventh-hour recitations that they couldn't cut. So Julia dashed into my room and begged me to walk him about the campus and then deliver him to her when the seventh hour was over. I said I would, obligingly but unenthusiastically, because I don't care much for Pendletons.

But he turned out to be a sweet lamb. He's a real human being--not a Pendleton at all. We had a beautiful time; I've longed for an uncle ever since. Do you mind pretending you're my uncle? I believe they're superior to grandmothers.

Mr. Pendleton reminded me a little of you, Daddy, as you were twenty years ago. You see I know you intimately, even if we haven't ever met!

He's tall and thinnish with a dark face all over lines, and the funniest underneath smile that never quite comes through but just wrinkles up the corners of his mouth. And he has a way of making you feel right off as though you'd known him a long time. He's very companionable.

We walked all over the campus from the quadrangle to the athletic grounds; then he said he felt weak and must have some tea. He proposed that we go to College Inn--it's just off the campus by the pine walk. I said we ought to go back for Julia and Sallie, but he said he didn't like to have his nieces drink too much tea; it made them nervous. So we just ran away and had tea and muffins and marmalade and ice-cream and cake at a nice little table out on the balcony. The inn was quite conveniently empty, this being the end of the month and allowances low.

We had the jolliest time! But he had to run for his train the minute he got back and he barely saw Julia at all. She was furious with me for taking him off; it seems he's an unusually rich and desirable uncle. It relieved my mind to find he was rich, for the tea and things cost sixty cents apiece.

This morning (it's Monday now) three boxes of chocolates came by express for Julia and Sallie and me. What do you think of that? To be getting candy from a man!

I begin to feel like a girl instead of a foundling.

I wish you'd come and have tea some day and let me see if I like you. But wouldn't it be dreadful if I didn't? However, I know I should.

Bien! I make you my compliments.

'Jamais je ne t'oublierai.'

Judy

PS. I looked in the glass this morning and found a perfectly new dimple that I'd never seen before. It's very curious. Where do you suppose it came from?

9th June

Dear Daddy-Long-Legs,

Happy day! I've just finished my last examination Physiology. And now:

Three months on a farm!

I don't know what kind of a thing a farm is. I've never been on one in my life. I've never even looked at one (except from the car window), but I know I'm going to love it, and I'm going to love being FREE.

I am not used even yet to being outside the John Grier Home. Whenever I think of it excited little thrills chase up and down my back. I feel as though I must run faster and faster and keep looking over my shoulder to make sure that Mrs. Lippett isn't after me with her arm stretched out to grab me back.

I don't have to mind any one this summer, do I?

Your nominal authority doesn't annoy me in the least; you are too far away to do any harm. Mrs. Lippett is dead for ever, so far as I am concerned, and the Semples aren't expected to overlook my moral welfare, are they? No, I am sure not. I am entirely grown up. Hooray!

I leave you now to pack a trunk, and three boxes of teakettles and dishes and sofa cushions and books.

Yours ever,

Judy

PS. Here is my physiology exam. Do you think you could have passed?

LOCK WILLOW FARM,

Saturday night

Dearest Daddy-Long-Legs,

I've only just come and I'm not unpacked, but I can't wait to tell you how much I like farms. This is a heavenly, heavenly, HEAVENLY spot! The house is square like this: And OLD. A hundred years or so. It has a veranda on the side which I can't draw and a sweet porch in front. The picture really doesn't do it justice--those things that look like feather dusters are maple trees, and the prickly ones that border the drive are murmuring pines and hemlocks. It stands on the top of a hill and looks way off over miles of green meadows to another line of hills.

That is the way Connecticut goes, in a series

of Marcelle waves; and Lock Willow Farm is just on the crest of one wave. The barns used to be across the road where they obstructed the view, but a kind flash of lightning came from heaven and burnt them down.

The people are Mr. and Mrs. Semple and a hired girl and two hired men. The hired people eat in the kitchen, and the Semples and Judy in the dining-room. We had ham and eggs and biscuits and honey and jelly-cake and pie and pickles and cheese and tea for supper--and a great deal of conversation. I have never been so entertaining in my life; everything I say appears to be funny. I suppose it is, because I've never been in the country before, and my questions are backed by an all-inclusive ignorance.

The room marked with a cross is not where the murder was committed, but the one that I occupy. It's big and square and empty, with adorable old-fashioned furniture and windows that have to be propped up on sticks and green shades trimmed with gold that fall down if you touch them. And a big square mahogany table-- I'm going to spend the summer with my elbows spread out on it, writing a novel.

Oh, Daddy, I'm so excited! I can't wait till daylight to explore. It's 8.30 now, and I am about to blow out my candle and try to go to sleep. We rise at five. Did you ever know such fun? I can't believe this is really Judy. You and the Good Lord give me more than I deserve. I must be a very, very, VERY good person to pay. I'm going to be. You'll see.

Good night,

Judy

PS. You should hear the frogs sing and the little pigs squeal and you should see the new moon! I saw it over my right shoulder.

LOCK WILLOW,

12th July

Dear Daddy-Long-Legs,

How did your secretary come to know about Lock Willow? (That isn't a rhetorical question. I am awfully curious to know.) For listen to this: Mr. Jervis Pendleton used to own this farm, but now he has given it to Mrs. Semple who was his old nurse. Did you ever hear of such a funny coincidence? She still calls him 'master Jervie' and talks about what a sweet little boy he used to be. She has one of his baby curls put away in a box, and it is red--or at least reddish!

Since she discovered that I know him, I have risen very much in her opinion. Knowing a member of the Pendleton family is the best introduction one can have at Lock Willow. And the cream of the whole family is Master Jervis--I am pleased to say that Julia belongs to an inferior branch.

The farm gets more and more entertaining. I rode on a hay wagon yesterday. We have three big pigs and nine little piglets, and you should see them eat. They are pigs! We've oceans of little baby chickens and ducks and turkeys and guinea fowls. You must be mad to live in a city when you might live on a farm.

It is my daily business to hunt the eggs. I fell off a beam in the barn loft yesterday, while I was trying to crawl over to a nest that the black hen has stolen. And when I came in with a scratched knee, Mrs. Semple bound it up with witch-hazel, murmuring all the time, 'dear! Dear! It seems only yesterday that Master Jervie fell off that very same beam and scratched this very same knee.'

The scenery around here is perfectly beautiful. There's a valley and a river and a lot of wooded hills, and way in the distance a tall blue mountain that simply melts in your mouth.

We churn twice a week; and we keep the cream in the spring house which is made of stone with the brook running underneath. Some of the farmers around here have a separator, but we don't care for these new-fashioned ideas. It may be a little harder to separate the cream in pans, but it's sufficiently better to pay. We have six calves; and I've chosen the names for all of them.

1. Sylvia, because she was born in the woods.
2. Lesbia, after the Lesbia in Catullus.
3. Sallie.
4. Julia--a spotted, nondescript animal.
5. Judy, after me.
6. Daddy-Long-Legs. You don't mind, do you, Daddy? He's pure Jersey and has a sweet disposition. He looks like this--you can see how appropriate the name is.

I haven't had time yet to begin my immortal novel; the farm keeps me too busy.

Yours always,

Judy

PS. I've learned to make doughnuts.

PS. (2) If you are thinking of raising chickens, let me recommend Buff Orpingtons. They haven't any pin feathers.

PS. (3) I wish I could send you a pat of the nice, fresh butter I churned yesterday. I'm a fine dairy-maid!

PS. (4) This is a picture of Miss Jerusha Abbott, the future great author, driving home the cows.

Sunday

Dear Daddy-Long-Legs,

Isn't it funny? I started to write to you yesterday afternoon, but as far as I got was the heading, 'dear Daddy-Long-Legs', and then I remembered I'd promised to pick some blackberries for supper, so I went off and left the sheet lying on the table, and when I came back today, what do you think I found sitting in the middle

of the page? A real true Daddy-Long-Legs!

I picked him up very gently by one leg, and dropped him out of the window. I wouldn't hurt one of them for the world. They always remind me of you.

We hitched up the spring wagon this morning and drove to the Centre to church. It's a sweet little white frame church with a spire and three Doric columns in front (or maybe Ionic--I always get them mixed).

A nice sleepy sermon with everybody drowsily waving palm-leaf fans, and the only sound, aside from the minister, the buzzing of locusts in the trees outside. I didn't wake up till I found myself on my feet singing the hymn, and then I was awfully sorry I hadn't listened to the sermon; I should like to know more of the psychology of a man who would pick out such a hymn. This was it:

Come, leave your sports and earthly toys
And join me in celestial joys.
Or else, dear friend, a long farewell.
I leave you now to sink to hell.

I find that it isn't safe to discuss religion with the Semples. Their God (whom they have inherited intact from their remote Puritan ancestors) is a narrow, irrational, unjust, mean, revengeful, bigoted Person. Thank heaven I don't inherit God from anybody! I am free to make mine up as I wish Him. He's kind and sympathetic and imaginative and forgiving and understanding-- and He has a sense of humour.
I like the Semples immensely; their practice is so superior to their theory. They are better

than their own God. I told them so--and they are horribly troubled. They think I am blasphemous--and I think they are! We've dropped theology from our conversation.

This is Sunday afternoon.

Amasai (hired man) in a purple tie and some bright yellow buckskin gloves, very red and shaved, has just driven off with Carrie (hired girl) in a big hat trimmed with red roses and a blue muslin dress and her hair curled as tight as it will curl. Amasai spent all the morning washing the buggy; and Carrie stayed home from church ostensibly to cook the dinner, but really to iron the muslin dress.

In two minutes more when this letter is finished I am going to settle down to a book which I found in the attic. It's entitled, On the Trail, and sprawled across the front page in a funny little-boy hand:

Jervis Pendleton

if this book should ever roam,
Box its ears and send it home.

He spent the summer here once after he had been ill, when he was about eleven years old; and he left On the Trail behind. It looks well read--the marks of his grimy little hands are frequent! Also in a corner of the attic there is a water wheel and a windmill and some bows and arrows. Mrs. Semple talks so constantly about him that I begin to believe he really lives--not a grown man with a silk hat and walking stick, but a nice, dirty, tousle-headed boy who clatters up the stairs with an awful racket, and leaves the screen doors open, and is always asking for cookies. (And getting them, too, if I know Mrs. Semple!) He seems to have been an adventurous little soul--and brave and truthful. I'm sorry to think he is a Pendleton; he was meant for something better.

We're going to begin threshing oats tomorrow; a steam engine is coming and three extra men.

It grieves me to tell you that Buttercup (the spotted cow with one horn, Mother of Lesbia) has done a disgraceful thing. She got into the orchard Friday evening and ate apples under the trees, and ate and ate until they went to her head. For two days she has been perfectly dead drunk! That is the truth I am telling. Did you ever hear anything so scandalous?

Sir, I remain,

Your affectionate orphan,

Judy Abbott

PS. Indians in the first chapter and highwaymen in the second. I hold my breath. What can the third contain? 'red Hawk leapt twenty feet in the air and bit the dust.' That is the subject of the frontispiece. Aren't Judy and Jervie having fun?

15th September

Dear Daddy,

I was weighed yesterday on the flour scales in the general store at the Comers. I've gained nine pounds! Let me recommend Lock Willow as a health resort.

Yours ever,

Judy

25th September

Dear Daddy-Long-Legs,

Behold me--a Sophomore! I came up last Friday, sorry to leave Lock Willow, but glad to see the campus again. It is a pleasant sensation to come back to something familiar. I am beginning to feel at home in college, and in command of the situation; I am beginning, in fact, to feel at home in the world--as though I really belonged to it and had not just crept in on sufferance.

I don't suppose you understand in the least what I am trying to say. A person important enough to be a Trustee can't appreciate the feelings of a person unimportant enough to be a foundling.

And now, Daddy, listen to this. Whom do you think I am rooming with? Sallie McBride and Julia Rutledge Pendleton. It's the truth. We have a study and three little bedrooms--VOILA!

Sallie and I decided last spring that we should like to room together, and Julia made up her mind to stay with Sallie--why, I can't imagine, for they are not a bit alike; but the Pendletons are naturally conservative and inimical (fine word!) to change. Anyway, here we are. Think of Jerusha Abbott, late of the John Grier Home for Orphans, rooming with a Pendleton. This is a democratic country.

Sallie is running for class president, and unless all signs fail, she is going to be elected. Such an atmosphere of intrigue you should see what politicians we are! Oh, I tell you, Daddy, when we women get our rights, you men will have to look alive in order to keep yours. Election comes next Saturday, and we're going to have a torchlight procession in the evening, no matter who wins.

I am beginning chemistry, a most unusual study. I've never seen anything like it before. Molecules and Atoms are the material employed, but I'll be in a position to discuss them more definitely next month.

I am also taking argumentation and logic.

Also history of the whole world.

Also plays of William Shakespeare.

Also French.

If this keeps up many years longer, I shall become quite intelligent.

I should rather have elected economics than French, but I didn't dare, because I was afraid that unless I re-elected French, the Professor would not let me pass--as it was, I just managed to squeeze through the June examination. But I will say that my high-school preparation was not very adequate.

There's one girl in the class who chatters away in French as fast as she does in English. She went abroad with her parents when she was a child, and spent three years in a convent school. You can imagine how bright she is compared with the rest of us--irregular verbs are mere playthings. I wish my parents had chucked me into a French convent when I was little instead of a foundling asylum. Oh no, I don't either! Because then maybe I should never have known you. I'd rather know you than French.

Goodbye, Daddy. I must call on Harriet Martin now, and, having discussed the chemical situation, casually drop a few thoughts on the subject of our next president.

Yours in politics,

J. Abbott

17th October

Dear Daddy-Long-Legs,

Supposing the swimming tank in the gymnasium were filled full of lemon jelly, could a person trying to swim manage to keep on top or would he sink?

We were having lemon jelly for dessert when the question came up. We discussed it heatedly for half an hour and it's still unsettled. Sallie thinks that she could swim in it, but I am perfectly sure that the best swimmer in the world would sink. Wouldn't it be funny to be drowned in lemon jelly?

Two other problems are engaging the attention of our table.

1st. What shape are the rooms in an octagon house? Some of the girls insist that they're square; but I think they'd have to be shaped like a piece of pie. Don't you?

2nd. Suppose there were a great big hollow sphere made of looking-glass and you were sitting inside. Where would it stop reflecting your face and begin reflecting your back? The more one thinks about this problem, the more puzzling it becomes. You can see with what deep philosophical reflection we engage our leisure!

Did I ever tell you about the election? It happened three weeks ago, but so fast do we live, that three weeks is ancient history. Sallie was elected, and we had a torchlight parade with transparencies saying, 'mcBride for Ever,' and a band consisting of fourteen pieces (three mouth organs and eleven combs).

We're very important persons now in '258.' Julia and I come in for a great deal of reflected

glory. It's quite a social strain to be living in the same house with a president.

Bonne nuit, cher Daddy.

Acceptez mez compliments,

Tres respectueux,

je suis,

Votre Judy

12th November

Dear Daddy-Long-Legs,

We beat the Freshmen at basket ball yesterday. Of course we're pleased--but oh, if we could only beat the juniors! I'd be willing to be black and blue all over and stay in bed a week in a witch-hazel compress.

Sallie has invited me to spend the Christmas vacation with her. She lives in Worcester, Massachusetts. Wasn't it nice of her? I shall love to go. I've never been in a private family in my life, except at Lock Willow, and the Semples were grown-up and old and don't count. But the McBrides have a houseful of children (anyway two or three) and a mother and father and grandmother, and an Angora cat. It's a perfectly complete family! Packing your trunk and going away is more fun than staying behind. I am terribly excited at the prospect.

Seventh hour--I must run to rehearsal. I'm to be in the Thanksgiving theatricals. A prince in a tower with a velvet tunic and yellow curls. Isn't that a lark?

Yours,

J. A.

Saturday

Do you want to know what I look like? Here's a photograph of all three that Leonora Fenton took.

The light one who is laughing is Sallie, and the tall one with her nose in the air is Julia, and the little one with the hair blowing across her face is Judy--she is really more beautiful than that, but the sun was in her eyes.

'STONE GATE', WORCESTER, MASS.,
31st December

Dear Daddy-Long-Legs,

I meant to write to you before and thank you for your Christmas cheque, but life in the McBride household is very absorbing, and I don't seem able to find two consecutive minutes to spend at a desk.

I bought a new gown--one that I didn't need, but just wanted. My Christmas present this year is from Daddy-Long-Legs; my family just sent love.

I've been having the most beautiful vacation visiting Sallie. She lives in a big old-fashioned brick house with white trimmings set back from the street--exactly the kind of house that I used to look at so curiously when I was in the John Grier Home, and wonder what it could be like inside. I never expected to see with my own eyes--but here I am! Everything is so comfortable and restful and homelike; I walk from room to room and drink in the furnishings.

It is the most perfect house for children to be brought up in; with shadowy nooks for hide and seek, and open fire places for pop-corn, and an attic to romp in on rainy days and slippery banisters with a comfortable flat knob at the bottom, and a great big sunny kitchen, and a nice, fat, sunny cook who has lived in the family thirteen years and always saves out a piece of dough for the children to bake. Just the sight of such a house makes you want to be a child all over again.

And as for families! I never dreamed they could be so nice. Sallie has a father and mother and grandmother, and the sweetest three-year-old baby sister all over curls, and a medium-sized brother who always forgets to wipe his feet, and a big, good-looking brother named Jimmie, who is a junior at Princeton.

We have the jolliest times at the table--
everybody laughs and jokes and talks at once,
and we don't have to say grace beforehand. It's
a relief not having to thank Somebody for every
mouthful you eat. (I dare say I'm blasphemous;
but you'd be, too, if you'd offered as much obligatory thanks as I have.)

Such a lot of things we've done--I can't begin to tell you about them. Mr. McBride owns a
factory and Christmas eve he had a tree for the
employees' children. It was in the long packing-
room which was decorated with evergreens and
holly. Jimmie McBride was dressed as Santa
Claus and Sallie and I helped him distribute the
presents.

Dear me, Daddy, but it was a funny
sensation! I felt as benevolent as a Trustee of
the John Grier home. I kissed one sweet, sticky
little boy--but I don't think I patted any of them
on the head!

And two days after Christmas, they gave a

dance at their own house for ME.

It was the first really true ball I ever attended--college doesn't count where we dance with girls. I had a new white evening gown (your Christmas present--many thanks) and long white gloves and white satin slippers. The only drawback to my perfect, utter, absolute happiness was the fact that Mrs. Lippett couldn't see me leading the cotillion with Jimmie McBride. Tell her about it, please, the next time you visit the J. G. H.

Yours ever,

Judy Abbott

PS. Would you be terribly displeased, Daddy, if I didn't turn out to be a Great Author after all, but just a Plain Girl?

6.30, Saturday

Dear Daddy,

We started to walk to town today, but mercy!

how it poured. I like winter to be winter with snow instead of rain.

Julia's desirable uncle called again this afternoon--and brought a five-pound box of chocolates. There are advantages, you see, about rooming with Julia.

Our innocent prattle appeared to amuse him and he waited for a later train in order to take tea in the study. We had an awful lot of trouble getting permission. It's hard enough entertaining fathers and grandfathers, but uncles are a step worse; and as for brothers and cousins, they are next to impossible. Julia had to swear that he was her uncle before a notary public and then have the county clerk's certificate attached. (Don't I know a lot of law?) And even then I doubt if we could have had our tea if the Dean had chanced to see how youngish and good-looking Uncle Jervis is.

Anyway, we had it, with brown bread Swiss cheese sandwiches. He helped make them and then ate four. I told him that I had spent last summer at Lock Willow, and we had a beautiful gossipy time about the Semples, and the horses and cows and chickens. All the horses that he used to know are dead, except Grover, who was a baby colt at the time of his last visit--and poor Grove now is so old he can just limp about the pasture.

He asked if they still kept doughnuts in a yellow crock with a blue plate over it on the bottom shelf of the pantry--and they do! He wanted to know if there was still a woodchuck's hole under the pile of rocks in the night pasture--and there is! Amasai caught a big, fat, grey one there this summer, the twenty-fifth great-grandson of the one Master Jervis caught when he was a little boy.

I called him 'master Jervie' to his face, but he didn't appear to be insulted. Julia says she has never seen him so amiable; he's usually pretty unapproachable. But Julia hasn't a bit of tact; and men, I find, require a great deal. They purr if you rub them the right way and spit if you don't. (That isn't a very elegant metaphor. I mean it figuratively.)

We're reading Marie Bashkirtseff's journal. Isn't it amazing? Listen to this: 'Last night I was seized by a fit of despair that found utterance in moans, and that finally drove me to throw the dining-room clock into the sea.'

It makes me almost hope I'm not a genius; they must be very wearing to have about--and awfully destructive to the furniture.

Mercy! how it keeps Pouring. We shall have to swim to chapel tonight.

Yours ever,

Judy

20th Jan.

Dear Daddy-Long-Legs,

Did you ever have a sweet baby girl who was stolen from the cradle in infancy?

Maybe I am she! If we were in a novel, that would be the denouement, wouldn't it? It's really awfully queer not to know what one is--sort of exciting and romantic. There are such a lot of possibilities. Maybe I'm not American; lots of people aren't. I may be straight descended from the ancient Romans, or I may be a Viking's daughter, or I may be the child of a Russian exile and belong by rights in a Siberian prison, or maybe I'm a Gipsy--I think perhaps I am. I have a very WANDERING spirit, though I haven't as yet had much chance to develop it.

Do you know about that one scandalous blot in my career the time I ran away from the asylum because they punished me for stealing cookies? It's down in the books free for any Trustee to read. But really, Daddy, what could you expect? When you put a hungry little nine-year girl in the pantry scouring knives, with the cookie jar at her elbow, and go off and leave her alone; and then suddenly pop in again, wouldn't you expect to find her a bit crumby? And then when you jerk her by the elbow and box her ears, and make her leave the table when the pudding comes, and tell all the other children that it's because she's a thief, wouldn't you expect her to run away?

I only ran four miles. They caught me and brought me back; and every day for a week I was tied, like a naughty puppy, to a stake in the back yard while the other children were out at recess.

Oh, dear! There's the chapel bell, and after chapel I have a committee meeting. I'm sorry because I meant to write you a very entertaining letter this time.

Auf wiedersehen

Cher Daddy,

Pax tibi!

Judy

PS. There's one thing I'm perfectly sure of I'm not a Chinaman.

4th February

Dear Daddy-Long-Legs,

Jimmie McBride has sent me a Princeton banner as big as one end of the room; I am very grateful to him for remembering me, but I don't know what on earth to do with it. Sallie and Julia won't let me hang it up; our room this year is furnished in red, and you can imagine what an effect we'd have if I added orange and black. But it's such nice, warm, thick felt, I hate to waste it. Would it be very improper to have it made into a bath robe? My old one shrank when it was washed.

I've entirely omitted of late telling you what I am learning, but though you might not imagine it from my letters, my time is exclusively occupied with study. It's a very bewildering matter to get educated in five branches at once.

'the test of true scholarship,' says Chemistry Professor, 'is a painstaking passion for detail.'

'Be careful not to keep your eyes glued to

detail,' says History Professor. 'stand far enough away to get a perspective of the whole.'

You can see with what nicety we have to trim our sails between chemistry and history. I like the historical method best. If I say that William the Conqueror came over in 1492, and Columbus discovered America in 1100 or 1066 or whenever it was, that's a mere detail that the Professor overlooks. It gives a feeling of security and restfulness to the history recitation, that is entirely lacking in chemistry.

Sixth-hour bell--I must go to the laboratory and look into a little matter of acids and salts and alkalis. I've burned a hole as big as a plate in the front of my chemistry apron, with hydrochloric acid. If the theory worked, I ought to be able to neutralize that hole with good strong ammonia, oughtn't I?

Examinations next week, but who's afraid?

Yours ever,

Judy

5th March

Dear Daddy-Long-Legs,

There is a March wind blowing, and the sky is filled with heavy, black moving clouds. The crows in the pine trees are making such a clamour! It's an intoxicating, exhilarating, CALLING noise. You want to close your books and be off over the hills to race with the wind.

We had a paper chase last Saturday over five miles of squashy 'cross country. The fox (composed of three girls and a bushel or so of confetti) started half an hour before the twenty-seven hunters. I was one of the twenty-seven; eight dropped by the wayside; we ended nineteen. The trail led over a hill, through a cornfield, and into a swamp where we had to leap lightly from hummock to hummock. of course half of us went in ankle deep. We kept losing the trail, and we wasted twenty-five minutes over that swamp. Then up a hill through some woods and in at a barn window! The barn doors were all locked and the window was up high and pretty small. I don't call that fair, do you?

But we didn't go through; we circumnavigated the barn and picked up the trail where it issued by way of a low shed roof on to the top of a fence. The fox thought he had us there, but we fooled him. Then straight away over two miles of rolling meadow, and awfully hard to follow, for the confetti was getting sparse. The rule is that it must be at the most six feet apart, but they were the longest six feet I ever saw. Finally, after two hours of steady trotting, we tracked Monsieur Fox into the kitchen of Crystal Spring (that's a farm where the girls go in bob sleighs and hay wagons for chicken and waffle suppers) and we found the three foxes placidly eating milk and honey and biscuits. They hadn't thought we would get that far; they were expecting us to stick in the barn window.

Both sides insist that they won. I think we did, don't you? Because we caught them before they got back to the campus. Anyway, all nineteen of us settled like locusts over the furniture and clamoured for honey. There wasn't enough to go round, but Mrs. Crystal Spring (that's our pet name for her; she's by rights a Johnson) brought up a jar of strawberry jam and a can of maple syrup--just made last week--and three loaves of brown bread.

We didn't get back to college till half-past six--half an hour late for dinner--and we went straight in without dressing, and with perfectly unimpaired appetites! Then we all cut evening chapel, the state of our boots being enough of an excuse.

I never told you about examinations. I passed everything with the utmost ease--I know the secret now, and am never going to fail again. I shan't be able to graduate with honours though, because of that beastly Latin prose and geometry Freshman year. But I don't care. Wot's the hodds so long as you're 'appy? (That's a quotation. I've been reading the English classics.)

Speaking of classics, have you ever read Hamlet? If you haven't, do it right off. It's PERFECTLY CORKING. I've been hearing about Shakespeare all my life, but I had no idea he really wrote so well; I always suspected him of going largely on his reputation.

I have a beautiful play that I invented a long time ago when I first learned to read. I put myself to sleep every night by pretending I'm the person (the most important person) in the book I'm reading at the moment.

At present I'm Ophelia--and such a sensible Ophelia! I keep Hamlet amused all the time, and pet him and scold him and make him wrap up his throat when he has a cold. I've entirely cured him of being melancholy. The King and Queen are both dead--an accident at sea; no funeral necessary--so Hamlet and I are ruling in Denmark without any bother. We have the kingdom working beautifully. He takes care of the governing, and I look after the charities. I have just founded some first-class orphan asylums. If you or any of the other Trustees would like to visit them, I shall be pleased to show you through. I think you might find a great many helpful suggestions.

> *I remain, sir,*
> *Yours most graciously,*
> *OPHELIA,*
> *Queen of Denmark.*

24th March,

maybe the 25th

Dear Daddy-Long-Legs,

I don't believe I can be going to Heaven--I am getting such a lot of good things here; it wouldn't be fair to get them hereafter too. Listen to what has happened.

Jerusha Abbott has won the short-story contest (a twenty-five dollar prize) that the Monthly holds every year. And she's a Sophomore! The contestants are mostly Seniors. When I saw my name posted, I couldn't quite believe it was true. Maybe I am going to be an author after all. I wish Mrs. Lippett hadn't given me such a silly name--it sounds like an author-ess, doesn't it?

Also I have been chosen for the spring dramatics--As You Like It out of doors. I am going to be Celia, own cousin to Rosalind.

And lastly: Julia and Sallie and I are going to New York next Friday to do some spring shopping and stay all night and go to the theatre the next day with 'master Jervie.' He invited us. Julia is going to stay at home with her family, but Sallie and I are going to stop at the Martha Washington Hotel. Did you ever hear of anything so exciting? I've never been in a hotel in my life, nor in a theatre; except once when the Catholic Church had a festival and invited the orphans, but that wasn't a real play and it doesn't count.

And what do you think we're going to see?

Hamlet. Think of that! We studied it for four weeks in Shakespeare class and I know it by heart.

I am so excited over all these prospects that I can scarcely sleep.

Goodbye, Daddy.

This is a very entertaining world.

Yours ever,

Judy

PS. I've just looked at the calendar. It's the 28th.

Another postscript.

I saw a street car conductor today with one brown eye and one blue. Wouldn't he make a nice villain for a detective story?

7th April

Dear Daddy-Long-Legs,

Mercy! Isn't New York big? Worcester is nothing to it. Do you mean to tell me that you actually live in all that confusion? I don't believe that I shall recover for months from the bewildering effect of two days of it. I can't begin to tell you all the amazing things I've seen; I suppose you know, though, since you live there yourself.

But aren't the streets entertaining? And the people? And the shops? I never saw such lovely things as there are in the windows. It makes you want to devote your life to wearing clothes.
Sallie and Julia and I went shopping together Saturday morning. Julia went into the very most gorgeous place I ever saw, white and gold walls and blue carpets and blue silk curtains and gilt chairs. A perfectly beautiful lady with yellow hair and a long black silk trailing gown came to meet us with a welcoming smile. I thought we were paying a social call, and started to shake hands, but it seems we were only buying hats-- at least Julia was. She sat down in front of a mirror and tried on a dozen, each lovelier than the last, and bought the two loveliest of all.

I can't imagine any joy in life greater than sitting down in front of a mirror and buying any hat you choose without having first to consider the price! There's no doubt about it, Daddy; New York would rapidly undermine this fine stoical character which the John Grier Home so patiently built up.

And after we'd finished our shopping, we met Master Jervie at Sherry's. I suppose you've been in Sherry's? Picture that, then picture the dining-room of the John Grier Home with its oilcloth-covered tables, and white crockery that you CAN't break, and wooden-handled knives and forks; and fancy the way I felt!

I ate my fish with the wrong fork, but the waiter very kindly gave me another so that nobody noticed.

And after luncheon we went to the theatre--it was dazzling, marvellous, unbelievable--I dream about it every night.

Isn't Shakespeare wonderful?

Hamlet is so much better on the stage than when we analyze it in class; I appreciated it before, but now, clear me!

I think, if you don't mind, that I'd rather be an actress than a writer. Wouldn't you like me to leave college and go into a dramatic school? And then I'll send you a box for all my performances, and smile at you across the footlights. Only wear a red rose in your buttonhole, please, so I'll surely smile at the right man. It would be an awfully embarrassing mistake if I picked out the wrong one.

We came back Saturday night and had our dinner in the train, at little tables with pink lamps and negro waiters. I never heard of meals being served in trains before, and I inadvertently said so.

'Where on earth were you brought up?' said Julia to me.

'In a village,' said I meekly, to Julia.
'But didn't you ever travel?' said she to me.

'Not till I came to college, and then it was only a hundred and sixty miles and we didn't eat,' said I to her.

She's getting quite interested in me, because I say such funny things. I try hard not to, but they do pop out when I'm surprised--and I'm surprised most of the time. It's a dizzying experience, Daddy, to pass eighteen years in the John Grier Home, and then suddenly to be plunged into the WORLD.

But I'm getting acclimated. I don't make such awful mistakes as I did; and I don't feel uncomfortable any more with the other girls. I used to squirm whenever people looked at me. I felt as though they saw right through my sham new clothes to the checked ginghams underneath. But I'm not letting the ginghams bother me any more. Sufficient unto yesterday is the evil thereof.

I forgot to tell you about our flowers. Master Jervie gave us each a big bunch of violets and lilies-of-the-valley. Wasn't that sweet of him? I never used to care much for men--judging by Trustees--but I'm changing my mind.

Eleven pages--this is a letter! Have courage. I'm going to stop.

Yours always,

Judy

10th April

Dear Mr. Rich-Man,

Here's your cheque for fifty dollars. Thank you very much, but I do not feel that I can keep it. My allowance is sufficient to afford all of the hats that I need. I am sorry that I wrote all that silly stuff about the millinery shop; it's just that I had never seen anything like it before.

However, I wasn't begging! And I would rather not accept any more charity than I have to.

Sincerely yours,

Jerusha Abbott

11th April

Dearest Daddy,

Will you please forgive me for the letter I wrote you yesterday? After I posted it I was sorry, and tried to get it back, but that beastly mail clerk wouldn't give it back to me.

It's the middle of the night now; I've been awake for hours thinking what a Worm I am-- what a Thousand-legged Worm--and that's the worst I can say! I've closed the door very softly into the study so as not to wake Julia and Sallie, and am sitting up in bed writing to you on paper torn out of my history note-book.

I just wanted to tell you that I am sorry I was so impolite about your cheque. I know you meant it kindly, and I think you're an old dear to take so much trouble for such a silly thing as a hat. I ought to have returned it very much more graciously.

But in any case, I had to return it. It's different with me than with other girls. They can take things naturally from people. They have fathers and brothers and aunts and uncles; but I can't be on any such relations with any one. I like to pretend that you belong to me, just to play with the idea, but of course I know you don't. I'm alone, really--with my back to the wall fighting the world--and I get sort of gaspy when I think about it. I put it out of my mind, and keep on pretending; but don't you see, Daddy? I can't accept any more money than I have to, because some day I shall be wanting to pay it back, and even as great an author as I intend to be won't be able to face a PERFECTLY TREMENDOUS debt.

I'd love pretty hats and things, but I mustn't mortgage the future to pay for them.

You'll forgive me, won't you, for being so rude? I have an awful habit of writing impulsively when I first think things, and then posting the letter beyond recall. But if I sometimes seem thoughtless and ungrateful, I never mean it.

In my heart I thank you always for the life and freedom and independence that you have given me. My childhood was just a long, sullen stretch of revolt, and now I am so happy every moment of the day that I can't believe it's true. I feel like a made-up heroine in a story-book.

It's a quarter past two. I'm going to tiptoe out to post this off now. You'll receive it in the next mail after the other; so you won't have a very long time to think bad of me.

Good night, Daddy,

I love you always,

Judy

4th May

Dear Daddy-Long-Legs,

Field Day last Saturday. It was a very spectacular occasion. First we had a parade of all the classes, with everybody dressed in white linen, the Seniors carrying blue and gold Japanese

Judy Wins the Fifty Yard Dash

umbrellas, and the juniors white and yellow banners. Our class had crimson balloons--very fetching, especially as they were always getting loose and floating off--and the Freshmen wore green tissue-paper hats with long streamers. Also we had a band in blue uniforms hired from town. Also about a dozen funny people, like clowns in a circus, to keep the spectators entertained between events.

    Julia was dressed as a fat country man with a linen duster and whiskers and baggy umbrella. Patsy Moriarty (Patrici really. Did you ever hear such a name? Mrs. Lippett couldn't have done better) who is tall and thin was Julia's wife in a absurd green bonnet over one ear. Waves of laughter followed them the whole length of the course. Julia played the part extremely well. I never dreamed that a Pendleton could display so much comedy spirit--begging Master Jervie' pardon; I don't consider him a true Pendleton though, any more than I consider you a true Trustee.

Sallie and I weren't in the parade because we were entered for the events. And what do you think? We both won! At least in something. We tried for the running broad jump and lost; but Sallie won the pole-vaulting (seven feet three inches) and I won the fifty-yard sprint (eight seconds).

I was pretty panting at the end, but it was great fun, with the whole class waving balloons and cheering and yelling:

What's the matter with Judy Abbott?

She's all right.

Who's all right?

Judy Ab-bott!

That, Daddy, is true fame. Then trotting back to the dressing tent and being rubbed down with alcohol and having a lemon to suck. You see we're very professional. It's a fine thing to win an event for your class, because the class that wins the most gets the athletic cup for the year. The Seniors won it this year, with seven events to their credit. The athletic association gave a dinner in the gymnasium to all of the winners. We had fried soft-shell crabs, and chocolate ice-cream moulded in the shape of basket balls.

I sat up half of last night reading Jane Eyre. Are you old enough, Daddy, to remember sixty years ago? And, if so, did people talk that way? The haughty Lady Blanche says to the foot-man, 'stop your chattering, knave, and do my bidding.' Mr. Rochester talks about the metal welkin when he means the sky; and as for the mad woman who laughs like a hyena and sets

fire to bed curtains and tears up wedding veils
and BITES--it's melodrama of the purest, but
just the same, you read and read and read. I
can't see how any girl could have written such
a book, especially any girl who was brought up
in a churchyard. There's something about those
Brontes that fascinates me. Their books, their
lives, their spirit. Where did they get it? When
I was reading about little Jane's troubles in the
charity school, I got so angry that I had to go out
and take a walk. I understood exactly how she
felt. Having known Mrs. Lippett, I could see Mr.
Brocklehurst.

Don't be outraged, Daddy. I am not
intimating that the John Grier Home was like
the Lowood Institute. We had plenty to eat and
plenty to wear, sufficient water to wash in, and
a furnace in the cellar. But there was one deadly
likeness. Our lives were absolutely monotonous
and uneventful. Nothing nice ever happened,
except ice-cream on Sundays, and even that was

regular. In all the eighteen years I was there I only had one adventure--when the woodshed burned. We had to get up in the night and dress so as to be ready in case the house should catch. But it didn't catch and we went back to bed.

Everybody likes a few surprises; it's a perfectly natural human craving. But I never had one until Mrs. Lippett called me to the office to tell me that Mr. John Smith was going to send me to college. And then she broke the news so gradually that it just barely shocked me.

You know, Daddy, I think that the most necessary quality for any person to have is imagination. It makes people able to put themselves in other people's places. It makes them kind and sympathetic and understanding. It ought to be cultivated in children. But the John Grier Home instantly stamped out the slightest flicker that appeared. Duty was the one quality that was encouraged. I don't think children ought to know the meaning of the word; it's odious, detestable.

They ought to do everything from love.

Wait until you see the orphan asylum that I am going to be the head of! It's my favourite play at night before I go to sleep. I plan it out to the littlest detail--the meals and clothes and study and amusements and punishments; for even my superior orphans are sometimes bad.

But anyway, they are going to be happy. I think that every one, no matter how many troubles he may have when he grows up, ought to have a happy childhood to look back upon. And if I ever have any children of my own, no matter how unhappy I may be, I am not going to let them have any cares until they grow up.

(There goes the chapel bell--I'll finish this letter sometime).

Thursday

When I came in from laboratory this afternoon, I found a squirrel sitting on the tea table helping himself to almonds. These are the kind

of callers we entertain now that warm weather
has come and the windows stay open--

Saturday morning

Perhaps you think, last night being Friday, with no classes today, that I passed a nice quiet, readable evening with the set of Stevenson that I bought with my prize money? But if so, you've never attended a girls' college, Daddy dear. Six friends dropped in to make fudge, and one of them dropped the fudge--while it was still liquid--right in the middle of our best rug. We shall never be able to clean up the mess.

I haven't mentioned any lessons of late; but we are still having them every day. It's sort of a relief though, to get away from them and discuss life in the large--rather one-sided discussions that you and I hold, but that's your own fault. You are welcome to answer back any time you choose.

I've been writing this letter off and on for

three days, and I fear by now vous etes bien bored!

Goodbye, nice Mr. Man,

Judy Mr.

Daddy-Long-Legs Smith,

SIR: Having completed the study of argumentation and the science of dividing a thesis into heads, I have decided to adopt the following form for letter-writing. It contains all necessary facts, but no unnecessary verbiage.

I. We had written examinations this week in:

A. Chemistry.

B. History.

II. A new dormitory is being built.

A. Its material is:

(a) red brick.

(b) grey stone.

B. Its capacity will be:

(a) one dean, five instructors.

(b) two hundred girls.

(c) one housekeeper, three cooks, twenty waitresses, twenty chambermaids.

III. We had junket for dessert tonight.

IV. I am writing a special topic upon the Sources of Shakespeare's Plays.

V. Lou McMahon slipped and fell this afternoon at basket ball, and she:

    A. Dislocated her shoulder.

    B. Bruised her knee.

VI. I have a new hat trimmed with:

    A. Blue velvet ribbon.

    B. Two blue quills.

    C. Three red pompoms.

VII. It is half past nine.

VIII. Good night.

Judy

2nd June

Dear Daddy-Long-Legs,

You will never guess the nice thing that has

happened.

The McBrides have asked me to spend the summer at their camp in the Adirondacks! They belong to a sort of club on a lovely little lake in the middle of the woods. The different members have houses made of logs dotted about among the trees, and they go canoeing on the lake, and take long walks through trails to other camps, and have dances once a week in the club house--Jimmie McBride is going to have a college friend visiting him part of the summer, so you see we shall have plenty of men to dance with.

Wasn't it sweet of Mrs. McBride to ask me? It appears that she liked me when I was there for Christmas.

Please excuse this being short. It isn't a real letter; it's just to let you know that I'm disposed of for the summer.

Yours,

In a VERY contented

frame of mind,

Judy

5th June

Dear Daddy-Long-Legs,

Your secretary man has just written to me saying that Mr. Smith prefers that I should not accept Mrs. McBride's invitation, but should return to Lock Willow the same as last summer.

Why, why, WHY, Daddy?

You don't understand about it. Mrs. McBride does want me, really and truly. I'm not the least bit of trouble in the house. I'm a help. They don't take up many servants, and Sallie an I can do lots of useful things. It's a fine chance for me to learn housekeeping. Every woman ought to understand it, and I only know asylum-keeping.

There aren't any girls our age at the camp, and Mrs. McBride wants me for a companion for Sallie. We are planning to do a lot of reading together. We are going to read all of the books for next year's English and sociology. The Professor said it would be a great help if we would get our reading finished in the summer; and it's so much easier to remember it if we read together and talk it over.

Just to live in the same house with Sallie's mother is an education. She's the most interesting, entertaining, companionable, charming woman in the world; she knows everything. Think how many summers I've spent with Mrs. Lippett and how I'll appreciate the contrast. You needn't be afraid that I'll be crowding them, for their house is made of rubber. When they have a lot of company, they just sprinkle tents about in the woods and turn the boys outside. It's going to be such a nice, healthy summer exercising out of doors every minute. Jimmie McBride is going to teach me how to ride horseback and paddle a canoe, and how to shoot and--oh, lots of things I ought to know. It's the kind of nice, jolly, care-free time that I've never had; and I think every girl deserves it once in her life. Of course

I'll do exactly as you say, but please, PLEASE let me go, Daddy. I've never wanted anything so much.

This isn't Jerusha Abbott, the future great author, writing to you.

It's just Judy--a girl.

9th June

Mr. John Smith,

SIR: Yours of the 7th inst. at hand. In compliance with the instructions received through your secretary, I leave on Friday next to spend the summer at Lock Willow Farm.

I hope always to remain,

(Miss) Jerusha Abbott

LOCK WILLOW FARM,

3rd August

Dear Daddy-Long-Legs,

It has been nearly two months since I wrote, which wasn't nice of me, I know, but I haven't loved you much this summer--you see I'm being frank!

You can't imagine how disappointed I was at having to give up the McBrides' camp. Of course I know that you're my guardian, and that I have to regard your wishes in all matters, but I couldn't see any REASON. It was so distinctly the best thing that could have happened to me. If I had been Daddy, and you had been Judy, I should have said, 'Bless yo my child, run along and have a good time; see lots of new people and learn lots of new things; live out of doors, and get strong and well and rested for a year of hard work.'

But not at all! Just a curt line from your secretary ordering me to Lock Willow.

It's the impersonality of your commands that hurts my feelings. It seems as though, if you felt the tiniest little bit for me the way I feel for you, you'd sometimes send me a message that you'd written with your own hand, instead of those beastly typewritten secretary's notes. If there were the slightest hint that you cared, I'd do anything on earth to please you.

I know that I was to write nice, long, detailed letters without ever expecting any answer. You're living up to your side of the bargain--I'm being educated--and I suppose you're thinking I'm not living up to mine!

But, Daddy, it is a hard bargain. It is, really. I'm so awfully lonely. You are the only person I have to care for, and you are so shadowy. You're just an imaginary man that I've made up--and probably the real YOU isn't a bit like my imaginary YOU. But you did once, when I was ill in the infirmary, send me a message, and now, when I am feeling awfully forgotten, I get out your card and read it over.

I don't think I am telling you at all what I started to say, which was this:

Although my feelings are still hurt, for it is very humiliating to be picked up and moved about by an arbitrary, peremptory, unreasonable, omnipotent, invisible Providence, still, when a man has been as kind and generous and thoughtful as you have heretofore been towards me, I suppose he has a right to be an arbitrary, peremptory, unreasonable, invisible Providence if he chooses, and so--I'll forgive you and be cheerful again. But I still don't enjoy getting Sallie's letters about the good times they are having in camp!

However--we will draw a veil over that and begin again.

I've been writing and writing this summer; four short stories finished and sent to four different magazines. So you see I'm trying to be an author. I have a workroom fixed in a corner of the attic where Master Jervie used to have his rainy-day playroom. It's in a cool, breezy corner with two dormer windows, and shaded by a maple tree with a family of red squirrels living in a hole.

I'll write a nicer letter in a few days and tell you all the farm news.

We need rain.

Yours as ever,
Judy

10th August

Mr. Daddy-Long-Legs,

SIR: I address you from the second crotch in the willow tree by the pool in the pasture. There's a frog croaking underneath, a locust singing overhead and two little 'devil down-heads' darting up and down the trunk. I've been here for an hour; it's a very comfortable crotch, especially after being upholstered with two sofa cushions. I came up with a pen and tablet hoping to write an immortal short story, but I've been having a dreadful time with my heroine--I CAN't make her behave as I want her to behave; so I've abandoned her for the moment, and am writing to you. (Not much relief though, for I can't make you behave as I want you to, either.)

If you are in that dreadful New York, I wish I could send you some of this lovely, breezy, sunshiny outlook. The country is Heaven after a week of rain.

Speaking of Heaven--do you remember Mr. Kellogg that I told you about last summer?--the minister of the little white church at the Corners. Well, the poor old soul is dead--last winter of pneumonia. I went half a dozen times to hear him preach and got very well acquainted with his theology. He believed to the end exactly the same things he started with. It seems to me that a man who can think straight along for forty-seven years without changing a single idea ought to be kept in a cabinet as a curiosity. I hope he is enjoying his harp and golden crown; he was so perfectly sure of finding them! There's a new young man, very consequential, in his place. The congregation is pretty dubious, especially the faction led by Deacon Cummings.

It looks as though there was going to be an awful split in the church. We don't care for innovations in religion in this neighbourhood.

During our week of rain I sat up in the attic and had an orgy of reading--Stevenson, mostly. He himself is more entertaining than any of the characters in his books; I dare say he made himself into the kind of hero that would look well in print. Don't you think it was perfect of him to spend all the ten thousand dollars his father left, for a yacht, and go sailing off to the South Seas? He lived up to his adventurous creed. If my father had left me ten thousand dollars, I'd do it, too. The thought of Vailima makes me wild. I want to see the tropics. I want to see the whole world. I am going to be a great author, or artist, or actress, or playwright--or whatever sort of a great person I turn out to be. I have a terrible wanderthirst; the very sight of a map makes me want to put on my hat and take an umbrella and start. 'I shall see before I die the palms and temples of the South.'

**Thursday evening at twilight,
sitting on the doorstep.**

Very hard to get any news into this letter! Judy is becoming so philosophical of late, that she wishes to discourse largely of the world in general, instead of descending to the trivial details of daily life. But if you MUST have news, here it is:

Our nine young pigs waded across the brook and ran away last Tuesday, and only eight came

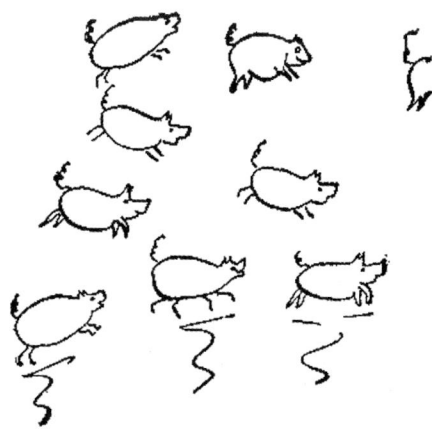

back. We don't want to accuse anyone unjustly, but we suspect that Widow Dowd has one more than she ought to have.

Mr. Weaver has painted his barn and his two silos a bright pumpkin yellow--a very ugly colour, but he says it will wear.

The Brewers have company this week; Mrs. Brewer's sister and two nieces from Ohio.

One of our Rhode Island Reds only brought off three chicks out of fifteen eggs. We can't imagine what was the trouble. Rhode island Reds, in my opinion, are a very inferior breed. I prefer Buff Orpingtons.

The new clerk in the post office at Bonnyrigg Four Corners drank every drop of Jamaica ginger they had in stock--seven dollars' worth--before he was discovered.

Old Ira Hatch has rheumatism and can't work any more; he never saved his money when he was earning good wages, so now he has to live on the town.

There's to be an ice-cream social at the schoolhouse next Saturday evening. Come and bring your families.

I have a new hat that I bought for twenty-five cents at the post office. This is my latest portrait, on my way to rake the hay.

It's getting too dark to see; anyway, the news is all used up.

Good night,

Judy

Friday

Good morning! Here is some news! What do you think? You'd never, never, never guess who's coming to Lock Willow. A letter to Mrs. Semple from Mr. Pendleton. He's motoring through the Berkshires, and is tired and wants to rest on a nice quiet farm--if he climbs out at her doorstep some night will she have a room ready for him? Maybe he'll stay one week, or maybe two, or maybe three; he'll see how restful it is when he gets here.

Such a flutter as we are in! The whole house is being cleaned and all the curtains washed. I am driving to the Corners this morning to get some new oilcloth for the entry, and two cans of brown floor paint for the hall and back stairs. Mrs. Dowd is engaged to come tomorrow to wash the windows (in the exigency of the moment, we waive our suspicions in regard to the piglet). You might think, from this account of our activities, that the house was not already immaculate; but I assure you it was! Whatever Mrs. Semple's limitations, she is a HOUSE-KEEPER.

But isn't it just like a man, Daddy? He doesn't give the remotest hint as to whether he will land on the doorstep today, or two weeks from today. We shall live in a perpetual breathlessness until he comes--and if he doesn't hurry, the cleaning may all have to be done over again.

There's Amasai waiting below with the

buckboard and Grover. I drive alone--but if you could see old Grove, you wouldn't be worried as to my safety.

With my hand on my heart--farewell.

Judy

PS. Isn't that a nice ending? I got it out of Stevenson's letters.

Saturday

Good morning again! I didn't get this ENVELOPED yesterday before the postman came, so I'll add some more. We have one mail a day at twelve o'clock. Rural delivery is a blessing to the farmers! Our postman not only delivers letters, but he runs errands for us in town, at five cents an errand. Yesterday he brought me some shoe-strings and a jar of cold cream (I sunburned all the skin off my nose before I got my new hat) and a blue Windsor tie and a bottle of blacking all for ten cents. That was an unusual bargain, owing to the largeness of my order.

Also he tells us what is happening in the Great World. Several people on the route take daily papers, and he reads them as he jogs along, and repeats the news to the ones who don't subscribe. So in case a war breaks out between the United States and Japan, or the president is assassinated, or Mr. Rockefeller leaves a million dollars to the John Grier Home, you needn't bother to write; I'll hear it anyway.

No sign yet of Master Jervie. But you should see how clean our house is--and with what anxiety we wipe our feet before we step in!

I hope he'll come soon; I am longing for someone to talk to. Mrs. Semple, to tell you the truth, gets rather monotonous. She never lets ideas interrupt the easy flow of her conversation. It's a funny thing about the people here. Their world is just this single hilltop. They are not a bit universal, if you know what I mean. It's exactly the same as at the John Grier Home. Our ideas there were bounded by the four sides of the iron fence, only I didn't mind it so much because I was younger, and was so awfully busy. By the time I'd got all my beds made and my babies' faces washed and had gone to school and come home and had washed their faces again and darned their stockings and mended Freddie Perkins's trousers (he tore them every day of his life) and learned my lessons in between--I was ready to go to bed, and I didn't notice any lack of social intercourse. But after two years in a conversational college, I do miss it; and I shall be glad to see somebody who speaks my language.

I really believe I've finished, Daddy. Nothing else occurs to me at the moment--I'll try to write a longer letter next time.

Yours always,

Judy

PS. The lettuce hasn't done at all well this year. It was so dry early in the season.

25th August

Well, Daddy, Master Jervie's here. And such a nice time as we're having! At least I am, and I think he is, too--he has been here ten days and he doesn't show any signs of going. The way Mrs. Semple pampers that man is scandalous. If she indulged him as much when he was a baby, I don't know how he ever turned out so well.

He and I eat at a little table set on the side porch, or sometimes under the trees, or--when it rains or is cold--in the best parlour. He just picks out the spot he wants to eat in and Carrie trots after him with the table. Then if it has been an awful nuisance, and she has had to carry the dishes very far, she finds a dollar under the sugar bowl.

He is an awfully companionable sort of man, though you would never believe it to see him casually; he looks at first glance like a true Pendleton, but he isn't in the least. He is just as simple and unaffected and sweet as he can be--that seems a funny way to describe a man, but it's true. He's extremely nice with the farmers around here; he meets them in a sort of man-to-man fashion that disarms them immediately. They were very suspicious at first. They didn't care for his clothes! And I will say that his clothes are rather amazing. He wears knickerbockers and pleated jackets and white flannels and riding clothes with puffed trousers. Whenever he comes down in anything new, Mrs. Semple, beaming with pride, walks around and views him from every angle, and urges him to be careful where he sits down; she is so afraid he will pick up some dust. It bores him dreadfully. He's always saying to her:

'Run along, Lizzie, and tend to your work. You can't boss me any longer. I've grown up.'

It's awfully funny to think of that great big, long-legged man (he's nearly as long-legged as you, Daddy) ever sitting in Mrs. Semple's lap and having his face washed. Particularly funny when you see her lap! She has two laps now, and three chins. But he says that once she was thin and wiry and spry and could run faster than he.

Such a lot of adventures we're having! We've explored the country for miles, and I've learned to fish with funny little flies made of feathers. Also to shoot with a rifle and a revolver. Also to ride horseback--there's an astonishing amount of life in old Grove. We fed him on oats for three days, and he shied at a calf and almost ran away with me.

Wednesday

We climbed Sky Hill Monday afternoon. That's a mountain near here; not an awfully high mountain, perhaps--no snow on the summit--but at least you are pretty breathless when you reach the top. The lower slopes are covered with woods, but the top is just piled rocks and open moor. We stayed up for the sunset and built a fire and cooked our supper.

Master Jervie did the cooking; he said he knew how better than me and he did, too, because he's used to camping. Then we came down by moonlight, and, when we reached the wood trail where it was dark, by the light of an electric bulb that he had in his pocket. It was such fun! He laughed and joked all the way and talked about interesting things. He's read all the books I've ever read, and a lot of others besides. It's astonishing how many different things he knows.

We went for a long tramp this morning and got caught in a storm. Our clothes were drenched before we reached home but our spirits not even damp. You should have seen Mrs. Semple's face when we dripped into her kitchen.

'Oh, Master Jervie--Miss Judy! You are soaked through. Dear! Dear! What shall I do? That nice new coat is perfectly ruined.'

She was awfully funny; you would have thought that we were ten years old, and she a distracted mother. I was afraid for a while that we weren't going to get any jam for tea.

Saturday

I started this letter ages ago, but I haven't had a second to finish it.

Isn't this a nice thought from Stevenson?

The world is so full of a number of things,
I am sure we should all be as happy as kings.

It's true, you know. The world is full of happiness, and plenty to go round, if you are only willing to take the kind that comes your way. The whole secret is in being PLIABLE. In the country, especially, there are such a lot of entertaining things. I can walk over everybody's land, and look at everybody's view, and dabble in everybody's brook; and enjoy it just as much as though I owned the land--and with no taxes to pay!

It's Sunday night now, about eleven o'clock, and I am supposed to be getting some beauty sleep, but I had black coffee for dinner, so--no beauty sleep for me!

This morning, said Mrs. Semple to Mr. Pendleton, with a very determined accent:

'We have to leave here at a quarter past ten in order to get to church by eleven.'

'very well, Lizzie,' said Master Jervie, 'you have the buggy ready, and if I'm not dressed, just go on without waiting.' 'We'll wait,' said she.

'As you please,' said he, 'only don't keep the horses standing too long.'

Then while she was dressing, he told Carrie to pack up a lunch, and he told me to scramble into my walking clothes; and we slipped out the back way and went fishing.

It discommoded the household dreadfully, because Lock Willow of a Sunday dines at two. But he ordered dinner at seven--he orders meals whenever he chooses; you would think the place were a restaurant--and that kept Carrie and Amasai from going driving. But he said it was all the better because it wasn't proper for them to go driving without a chaperon; and anyway, he wanted the horses himself to take me driving. Did you ever hear anything so funny?

And poor Mrs. Semple believes that people who go fishing on Sundays go afterwards to a sizzling hot hell! She is awfully troubled to think that she didn't train him better when he was small and helpless and she had the chance. Besides--she wished to show him off in church.

Anyway, we had our fishing (he caught four little ones) and we cooked them on a camp-fire for lunch. They kept falling off our spiked sticks into the fire, so they tasted a little ashy, but we ate them. We got home at four and went driving at five and had dinner at seven, and at ten I was sent to bed and here I am, writing to you.

I am getting a little sleepy, though.

Good night.

Here is a picture of the one fish I caught.

Ship Ahoy, Cap'n Long-Legs!

Avast! Belay! Yo, ho, ho, and a bottle of rum. Guess what I'm reading? Our conversation these past two days has been nautical and piratical. Isn't Treasure Island fun? Did you ever read it, or wasn't it written when you were a boy? Stevenson only got thirty pounds for the serial rights--I don't believe it pays to be a great author. Maybe I'll be a school-teacher.

Excuse me for filling my letters so full of Stevenson; my mind is very much engaged with him at present. He comprises Lock Willow's library.

I've been writing this letter for two weeks, and I think it's about long enough. Never say, Daddy, that I don't give details. I wish you were here, too; we'd all have such a jolly time together. I like my different friends to know each other. I wanted to ask Mr. Pendleton if he knew you in New York--I should think he might; you must move in about the same exalted social circles, and you are both interested in reforms and things--but I couldn't, for I don't know your real name.

It's the silliest thing I ever heard of, not to know your name. Mrs. Lippett warned me that you were eccentric. I should think so!

Affectionately,

Judy

PS. On reading this over, I find that it isn't all Stevenson. There are one or two glancing references to Master Jervie.

10th September

Dear Daddy,

He has gone, and we are missing him! When you get accustomed to people or places or ways of living, and then have them snatched away, it does leave an awfully empty, gnawing sort of sensation. I'm finding Mrs. Semple's conversation pretty unseasoned food.

College opens in two weeks and I shall be

glad to begin work again. I have worked quite a lot this summer though--six short stories and seven poems. Those I sent to the magazines all came back with the most courteous promptitude. But I don't mind. It's good practice. Master Jervie read them--he brought in the post, so I couldn't help his knowing--and he said they were DREADFUL. They showed that I didn't have the slightest idea of what I was talking about. (Master Jervie doesn't let politeness interfere with truth.) But the last one I did--just a little sketch laid in college--he said wasn't bad; and he had it typewritten, and I sent it to a magazine. They've had it two weeks; maybe they're thinking it over.

You should see the sky! There's the queerest orange-coloured light over everything. We're going to have a storm.

It commenced just that moment with tremendously big drops and all the shutters banging.

I had to run to close the windows, while Carrie flew to the attic with an armful of milk pans to put under the places where the roof leaks and then, just as I was resuming my pen, I remembered that I'd left a cushion and rug and hat and Matthew Arnold's poems under a tree in the orchard, so I dashed out to get them, all quite soaked. The red cover of the poems had run into the inside; Dover Beach in the future will be washed by pink waves.

A storm is awfully disturbing in the country. You are always having to think of so many things that are out of doors and getting spoiled.

Thursday

Daddy! Daddy! What do you think? The postman has just come with two letters.

1st. My story is accepted. $50.
ALORS! I'm an AUTHOR.
2nd. A letter from the college secretary. I'm to have a scholarship for two years that will cov-

er board and tuition. It was founded for 'marked proficiency in English with general excellency in other lines.' And I've won it! I applied for it before I left, but I didn't have an idea I'd get it, on account of my Freshman bad work in maths and Latin. But it seems I've made it up. I am awfully glad, Daddy, because now I won't be such a burden to you. The monthly allowance will be all I'll need, and maybe I can earn that with writing or tutoring or something.

I'm LONGING to go back and begin work.

Yours ever,

Jerusha Abbott,

Author of When the Sophomores Won the Game.

For sale at all news stands, price ten cents.

26th September

Dear Daddy-Long-Legs,

Back at college again and an upper classman. Our study is better than ever this year--faces the South with two huge windows and oh! so furnished. Julia, with an unlimited allowance, arrived two days early and was attacked with a fever for settling.

We have new wall paper and oriental rugs and mahogany chairs--not painted mahogany which made us sufficiently happy last year, but real. It's very gorgeous, but I don't feel as though I belonged in it; I'm nervous all the time for fear I'll get an ink spot in the wrong place.

And, Daddy, I found your letter waiting for me--pardon--I mean your secretary's.

Will you kindly convey to me a comprehensible reason why I should not accept that scholarship? I don't understand your objection in the least. But anyway, it won't do the slightest good for you to object, for I've already accepted it and I am not going to change! That sounds a little impertinent, but I don't mean it so.

I suppose you feel that when you set out to educate me, you'd like to finish the work, and put a neat period, in the shape of a diploma, at the end.

But look at it just a second from my point of view. I shall owe my education to you just as much as though I let you pay for the whole of it, but I won't be quite so much indebted. I know that you don't want me to return the money, but nevertheless, I am going to want to do it, if I possibly can; and winning this scholarship makes it so much easier. I was expecting to spend the rest of my life in paying my debts, but now I shall only have to spend one-half of the rest of it.

I hope you understand my position and won't be cross. The allowance I shall still most gratefully accept. It requires an allowance to live up to Julia and her furniture! I wish that she had been reared to simpler tastes, or else that she were not my room-mate.

This isn't much of a letter; I meant to have written a lot--but I've been hemming four window curtains and three portieres (I'm glad you can't see the length of the stitches), and polishing a brass desk set with tooth powder (very uphill work), and sawing off picture wire with manicure scissors, and unpacking four boxes of books, and putting away two trunkfuls of clothes (it doesn't seem believable that Jerusha Abbott owns two trunks full of clothes, but she does!) and welcoming back fifty dear friends in between.

Opening day is a joyous occasion!

Good night, Daddy dear, and don't be annoyed because your chick is wanting to scratch for herself. She's growing up into an awfully energetic little hen--with a very determined cluck and lots of beautiful feathers (all due to you).

Affectionately,

Judy

30th September

Dear Daddy,

Are you still harping on that scholarship? I never knew a man so obstinate, and stubborn and unreasonable, and tenacious, and bull-doggish, and unable-to-see-other-people's-point-of-view, as you.

You prefer that I should not be accepting favours from strangers.

Strangers!--And what are you, pray?

Is there anyone in the world that I know less? I shouldn't recognize you if I met you in the street. Now, you see, if you had been a sane, sensible person and had written nice, cheering fatherly letters to your little Judy, and had come occasionally and patted her on the head, and had said you were glad she was such a good girl--Then, perhaps, she wouldn't have flouted you in your old age, but would have obeyed your slightest wish like the dutiful daughter she was meant to be.

Strangers indeed! You live in a glass house,

Mr. Smith.

And besides, this isn't a favour; it's like a prize--I earned it by hard work. If nobody had been good enough in English, the committee wouldn't have awarded the scholarship; some years they don't. Also-- But what's the use of arguing with a man? You belong, Mr. Smith, to a sex devoid of a sense of logic. To bring a man into line, there are just two methods: one must either coax or be disagreeable. I scorn to coax men for what I wish. Therefore, I must be disagreeable.

I refuse, sir, to give up the scholarship; and if you make any more fuss, I won't accept the monthly allowance either, but will wear myself into a nervous wreck tutoring stupid Freshmen.

That is my ultimatum!

And listen--I have a further thought. Since you are so afraid that by taking this scholarship I am depriving someone else of an education, I know a way out. You can apply the money that you would have spent for me towards educating some other little girl from the John Grier Home. Don't you think that's a nice idea? Only, Daddy, EDUCATE the new girl as much as you choose, but please don't LIKE her any better than me.

I trust that your secretary won't be hurt because I pay so little attention to the suggestions offered in his letter, but I can't help it if he is. He's a spoiled child, Daddy. I've meekly given in to his whims heretofore, but this time I intend to be FIRM.

Yours, With a mind,

Completely and Irrevocably and

World-without-End Made-up,

Jerusha Abbott

9th November

Dear Daddy-Long-Legs,

I started down town today to buy a bottle of shoe blacking and some collars and the material for a new blouse and a jar of violet cream and a cake of Castile soap--all very necessary; I couldn't be happy another day without them--and when I tried to pay the car fare, I found that I had left my purse in the pocket of my other coat. So I had to get out and take the next car, and was late for gymnasium.

It's a dreadful thing to have no memory and two coats!

Julia Pendleton has invited me to visit her for the Christmas holidays. How does that strike you, Mr. Smith? Fancy Jerusha Abbott, of the John Grier Home, sitting at the tables of the rich. I don't know why Julia wants me--she seems to be getting quite attached to me of late. I should, to tell the truth, very much prefer going to Sallie's, but Julia asked me first, so if I go anywhere it must be to New York instead of to Worcester. I'm rather awed at the prospect of meeting Pendletons EN MASSE, and also I'd have to get a lot of new clothes--so, Daddy dear, if you write that you would prefer having me remain quietly at college, I will bow to your wishes with my usual sweet docility.

I'm engaged at odd moments with the Life and Letters of Thomas Huxley--it makes nice, light reading to pick up between times. Do you know what an archaeopteryx is? It's a bird. And a stereognathus? I'm not sure myself, but I think it's a missing link, like a bird with teeth or a lizard with wings. No, it isn't either; I've just looked in the book. It's a mesozoic mammal.

I've elected economics this year--very illuminating subject. When I finish that I'm going to take Charity and Reform; then, Mr. Trustee, I'll know just how an orphan asylum ought to be run. Don't you think I'd make an admirable voter if I had my rights? I was twenty-one last week. This is an awfully wasteful country to throw away such an honest, educated, conscientious, intelligent citizen as I would be.

Yours always,

Judy

7th December

Dear Daddy-Long-Legs,

Thank you for permission to visit Julia--I take it that silence means consent.

Such a social whirl as we've been having! The Founder's dance came last week--this was the first year that any of us could attend; only upper classmen being allowed.

I invited Jimmie McBride, and Sallie invited his room-mate at Princeton, who visited them last summer at their camp--an awfully nice man with red hair--and Julia invited a man from New York, not very exciting, but socially irreproachable. He is connected with the De la Mater Chichesters. Perhaps that means something to you? It doesn't illuminate me to any extent.

However--our guests came Friday afternoon in time for tea in the senior corridor, and then dashed down to the hotel for dinner. The hotel was so full that they slept in rows on the billiard tables, they say. Jimmie McBride says that the next time he is bidden to a social event in this college, he is going to bring one of their Adirondack tents and pitch it on the campus.

At seven-thirty they came back for the President's reception and dance. Our functions commence early! We had the men's cards all made out ahead of time, and after every dance, we'd leave them in groups, under the letter that stood for their names, so that they could be readily found by their next partners. Jimmie McBride, for example, would stand patiently under 'm' until he was claimed. (At least, he ought to have stood patiently, but he kept wandering off and getting mixed with 'R's' and 's's' and all sorts of letters.) I found him a very difficult guest; he was sulky because he had only three dances with me. He said he was bashful about dancing with girls he didn't know!

The next morning we had a glee club concert--and who do you think wrote the funny new song composed for the occasion? It's the truth. She did. Oh, I tell you, Daddy, your little foundling is getting to be quite a prominent person!

Anyway, our gay two days were great fun, and I think the men enjoyed it. Some of them were awfully perturbed at first at the prospect of facing one thousand girls; but they got acclimated very quickly. Our two Princeton men had a beautiful time--at least they politely said they had, and they've invited us to their dance next spring. We've accepted, so please don't object, Daddy dear.

Julia and Sallie and I all had new dresses. Do you want to hear about them? Julia's was cream satin and gold embroidery and she wore purple orchids. It was a DREAM and came from Paris, and cost a million dollars.

Sallie's was pale blue trimmed with Persian embroidery, and went beautifully with red hair. It didn't cost quite a million, but was just as effective as Julia's.

Mine was pale pink crepe de chine trimmed with ecru lace and rose satin. And I carried crimson roses which J. McB. sent (Sallie having told him what colour to get). And we all had satin slippers and silk stockings and chiffon scarfs to match.

You must be deeply impressed by these millinery details.

One can't help thinking, Daddy, what a colourless life a man is forced to lead, when one reflects that chiffon and Venetian point and hand embroidery and Irish crochet are to him mere empty words. Whereas a woman--whether she is interested in babies or microbes or husbands or poetry or servants or parallelograms or gardens or Plato or bridge--is fundamentally and always interested in clothes.

It's the one touch of nature that makes the whole world kin. (That isn't original. I got it out of one of Shakespeare's plays).

However, to resume. Do you want me to tell

you a secret that I've lately discovered? And will you promise not to think me vain? Then listen:

I'm pretty.

I am, really. I'd be an awful idiot not to know it with three looking-glasses in the room.

A Friend

PS. This is one of those wicked anonymous letters you read about in novels.

20th December

Dear Daddy-Long-Legs,

I've just a moment, because I must attend two classes, pack a trunk and a suit-case, and catch the four-o'clock train--but I couldn't go without sending a word to let you know how much I appreciate my Christmas box.

I love the furs and the necklace and the Liberty scarf and the gloves and handkerchiefs and books and purse--and most of all I love you! But Daddy, you have no business to spoil me this way. I'm only human--and a girl at that. How can I keep my mind sternly fixed on a studious career, when you deflect me with such worldly frivolities?

I have strong suspicions now as to which one of the John Grier Trustees used to give the Christmas tree and the Sunday ice-cream. He was nameless, but by his works I know him! You deserve to be happy for all the good things you do.

Goodbye, and a very merry Christmas.

Yours always,

Judy

PS. I am sending a slight token, too. Do you think you would like her if you knew her?

11th January

I meant to write to you from the city, Daddy, but New York is an engrossing place.

I had an interesting--and illuminating--time, but I'm glad I don't belong to such a family! I should truly rather have the John Grier Home for a background. Whatever the drawbacks of my bringing up, there was at least no pretence about it. I know now what people mean when they say they are weighed down by Things. The material atmosphere of that house was crushing; I didn't draw a deep breath until I was on an express train coming back. All the furniture was carved and upholstered and gorgeous; the people I met were beautifully dressed and low-voiced and well-bred, but it's the truth, Daddy, I never heard one word of real talk from the time we arrived until we left. I don't think an idea ever entered the front door.

Mrs. Pendleton never thinks of anything but jewels and dressmakers and social engagements. She did seem a different kind of mother from Mrs. McBride! If I ever marry and have a family, I'm going to make them as exactly like the McBrides as I can. Not for all the money in the world would I ever let any children of mine develop into Pendletons. Maybe it isn't polite to criticize people you've been visiting? If it isn't, please excuse. This is very confidential, between you and me.

I only saw Master Jervie once when he called at tea time, and then I didn't have a chance to speak to him alone. It was really disappointing after our nice time last summer. I don't think he cares much for his relatives--and I am sure they don't care much for him! Julia's mother says he's unbalanced. He's a Socialist--except, thank Heaven, he doesn't let his hair grow and wear red ties. She can't imagine where he picked up his queer ideas; the family have been Church of England for generations. He throws away his money on every sort of crazy reform, instead of spending it on such sensible things as yachts and automobiles and polo ponies. He does buy candy with it though! He sent Julia and me each a box for Christmas.

You know, I think I'll be a Socialist, too. You wouldn't mind, would you, Daddy? They're quite different from Anarchists; they don't believe in blowing people up. Probably I am one by rights; I belong to the proletariat. I haven't determined yet just which kind I am going to be. I will look into the subject over Sunday, and declare my principles in my next.

I've seen loads of theatres and hotels and beautiful houses. My mind is a confused jumble of onyx and gilding and mosaic floors and palms. I'm still pretty breathless but I am glad to get back to college and my books--I believe that I really am a student; this atmosphere of academic calm I find more bracing than New York. College is a very satisfying sort of life; the books and study and regular classes keep you alive mentally, and then when your mind gets tired, you have the gymnasium and outdoor athletics, and always plenty of congenial friends who are thinking about the same things you are. We spend a whole evening in nothing but talk--talk--talk--and go to bed with a very uplifted feeling, as though we had settled permanently some pressing world problems. And filling in every crevice, there is always such a lot of nonsense--just silly jokes about the little things that come up but very satisfying. We do appreciate our own witticisms!

It isn't the great big pleasures that count the most; it's making a great deal out of the little ones--I've discovered the true secret of happiness, Daddy, and that is to live in the now. Not to be for ever regretting the past, or anticipating the future; but to get the most that you can out of this very instant. It's like farming. You can have extensive farming and intensive farming; well, I am going to have intensive living after this. I'm going to enjoy every second, and I'm going to KNOW I'm enjoying it while I'm enjoying it. Most people don't live; they just race. They are trying to reach some goal far away on the horizon, and in the heat of the going they get so breathless and panting that they lose all sight of the beautiful, tranquil country they are passing through; and then the first thing they know, they are old and worn out, and it doesn't make any difference whether they've reached the goal or not. I've decided to sit down by the way and pile up a lot of little happinesses, even if I never become a Great Author. Did you ever know such a philosopheress as I am developing into?

Yours ever,

Judy

PS. It's raining cats and dogs tonight. Two puppies and a kitten have just landed on the window-sill.

Dear Comrade,

Hooray! I'm a Fabian.

That's a Socialist who's willing to wait. We don't want the social revolution to come tomorrow morning; it would be too upsetting. We want it to come very gradually in the distant future, when we shall all be prepared and able to sustain the shock.

In the meantime, we must be getting ready, by instituting industrial, educational and orphan asylum reforms.

Yours, with fraternal love,

Judy

Monday, 3rd hour

11th February

Dear D.-L.-L.,

Don't be insulted because this is so short. It isn't a letter; it's just a LINE to say that I'm going to write a letter pretty soon when examinations are over. It is not only necessary that I pass, but pass WELL. I have a scholarship to live up to.

Yours, studying hard,

J. A.

5th March

Dear Daddy-Long-Legs,

President Cuyler made a speech this evening about the modern generation being flippant and superficial. He says that we are losing the old ideals of earnest endeavour and true scholarship; and particularly is this falling-off noticeable in our disrespectful attitude towards organized authority. We no longer pay a seemly deference to our superiors.

I came away from chapel very sober.

Am I too familiar, Daddy? Ought I to treat you with more dignity and aloofness?--Yes, I'm sure I ought. I'll begin again.

My Dear Mr. Smith,

You will be pleased to hear that I passed successfully my mid-year examinations, and am now commencing work in the new semester. I am leaving chemistry--having completed the course in qualitative analysis--and am entering upon the study of biology. I approach this subject with some hesitation, as I understand that we dissect angleworms and frogs.

An extremely interesting and valuable lecture was given in the chapel last week upon Roman Remains in Southern France. I have never listened to a more illuminating exposition of the subject.

We are reading Wordsworth's Tintern Abbey in connection with our course in English Literature. What an exquisite work it is, and how adequately it embodies his conceptions of Pantheism! The Romantic movement of the early part of the last century, exemplified in the works of such poets as Shelley, Byron, Keats, and Wordsworth, appeals to me very much more than the Classical period that preceded it. Speaking of poetry, have you ever read that charming little thing of Tennyson's called Locksley Hall?

I am attending gymnasium very regularly of late. A proctor system has been devised, and failure to comply with the rules causes a great deal of inconvenience. The gymnasium is equipped with a very beautiful swimming tank of cement and marble, the gift of a former graduate. My room-mate, Miss McBride, has given me her bathing-suit (it shrank so that she can no longer wear it) and I am about to begin swimming lessons.

We had delicious pink ice-cream for dessert last night. Only vegetable dyes are used in colouring the food. The college is very much opposed, both from aesthetic and hygienic motives, to the use of aniline dyes.

The weather of late has been ideal--bright sunshine and clouds interspersed with a few welcome snow-storms. I and my companions have enjoyed our walks to and from classes--particularly from.

Trusting, my dear Mr. Smith, that this will find you in your usual good health,

I remain,

Most cordially yours,
Jerusha Abbott

24th April

Dear Daddy,

Spring has come again! You should see how lovely the campus is. I think you might come and look at it for yourself. Master Jervie dropped in again last Friday--but he chose a most unpropitious time, for Sallie and Julia and I were just running to catch a train. And where do you think we were going? To Princeton, to attend a dance and a ball game, if you please! I didn't ask you if I might go, because I had a feeling that your secretary would say no. But it was entirely regular; we had leave-of-absence from college, and Mrs. McBride chaperoned us. We had a charming time--but I shall have to omit details; they are too many and complicated.

Saturday

Up before dawn! The night watchman called us--six of us--and we made coffee in a chafing dish (you never saw so many grounds!) and

walked two miles to the top of One Tree Hill to see the sun rise. We had to scramble up the last slope! The sun almost beat us! And perhaps you think we didn't bring back appetites to breakfast!

Dear me, Daddy, I seem to have a very ejaculatory style today; this page is peppered with exclamations.

I meant to have written a lot about the budding trees and the new cinder path in the athletic field, and the awful lesson we have in biology for tomorrow, and the new canoes on the lake, and Catherine Prentiss who has pneumonia, and Prexy's Angora kitten that strayed from home and has been boarding in Fergussen Hall for two weeks until a chambermaid reported it, and about my three new dresses--white and pink and blue polka dots with a hat to match--but I am too sleepy. I am always making this an excuse, am I not? But a girls' college is a busy place and we do get tired by the end of the day! Particularly when the day begins at dawn.

Affectionately,

Judy

15th May

Dear Daddy-Long-Legs,

Is it good manners when you get into a car just to stare straight ahead and not see anybody else?

A very beautiful lady in a very beautiful velvet dress got into the car today, and without the slightest expression sat for fifteen minutes and looked at a sign advertising suspenders.

It doesn't seem polite to ignore everybody else as though you were the only important person present. Anyway, you miss a lot. While she was absorbing that silly sign, I was studying a whole car full of interesting human beings.

The accompanying illustration is hereby reproduced for the first time. It looks like a spider on the end of a string, but it isn't at all; it's a picture of me learning to swim in the tank in the gymnasium.

The instructor hooks a rope into a ring in the back of my belt, and runs it through a pulley in the ceiling. It would be a beautiful system if one had perfect confidence in the probity of one's instructor. I'm always afraid, though, that she will let the rope get slack, so I keep one anxious eye on her and swim with the other, and with this divided interest I do not make the progress that I otherwise might.

Very miscellaneous weather we're having of late. It was raining when I commenced and now the sun is shining. Sallie and I are going out to play tennis--thereby gaining exemption from Gym.

A week later

I should have finished this letter long ago, but I didn't. You don't mind, do you, Daddy, if I'm not very regular? I really do love to write to you; it gives me such a respectable feeling of having some family. Would you like me to tell you something? You are not the only man to whom I write letters. There are two others! I have been receiving beautiful long letters this winter from Master Jervie (with typewritten envelopes so Julia won't recognize the writing). Did you ever hear anything so shocking? And every week or so a very scrawly epistle, usually on yellow tablet paper, arrives from Princeton. All of which I answer with business-like promptness. So you see--I am not so different from other girls--I get letters, too.

Did I tell you that I have been elected a member of the Senior Dramatic Club? Very recherche organization. Only seventy-five members out of one thousand. Do you think as a consistent Socialist that I ought to belong?

What do you suppose is at present engaging my attention in sociology? I am writing (figurez vous!) a paper on the Care of Dependent Children. The Professor shuffled up his subjects and dealt them out promiscuously, and that fell to me. C'est drole ca n'est pas?

There goes the gong for dinner. I'll post this as I pass the box.

Affectionately,

J.

4th June

Dear Daddy,

Very busy time--commencement in ten days, examinations tomorrow; lots of studying, lots of packing, and the outdoor world so lovely that it hurts you to stay inside.

But never mind, vacation's coming. Julia is going abroad this summer--it makes the fourth time. No doubt about it, Daddy, goods are not distributed evenly. Sallie, as usual, goes to the Adirondacks. And what do you think I am going to do? You may have three guesses. Lock Willow? Wrong. The Adirondacks with Sallie? Wrong. (I'll never attempt that again; I was discouraged last year.) Can't you guess anything else? You're not very inventive. I'll tell you, Daddy, if you'll promise not to make a lot of objections. I warn your secretary in advance that my mind is made up.

I am going to spend the summer at the seaside with a Mrs. Charles Paterson and tutor her daughter who is to enter college in the autumn. I met her through the McBrides, and she is a very charming woman. I am to give lessons in English and Latin to the younger daughter, too, but I shall have a little time to myself, and I shall be earning fifty dollars a month! Doesn't that impress you as a perfectly exorbitant amount? She offered it; I should have blushed to ask for more than twenty-five.

I finish at Magnolia (that's where she lives) the first of September, and shall probably spend the remaining three weeks at Lock Willow--I should like to see the Semples again and all the friendly animals.

How does my programme strike you, Daddy? I am getting quite independent, you see. You have put me on my feet and I think I can almost walk alone by now.

Princeton commencement and our examinations exactly coincide--which is an awful blow. Sallie and I did so want to get away in time for it, but of course that is utterly impossible.

Goodbye, Daddy. Have a nice summer and come back in the autumn rested and ready for another year of work. (That's what you ought to be writing to me!) I haven't any idea what you

do in the summer, or how you amuse yourself.
I can't visualize your surroundings. Do you play
golf or hunt or ride horseback or just sit in the
sun and meditate?

Anyway, whatever it is, have a good time and
don't forget Judy.

10th June

Dear Daddy,

This is the hardest letter I ever wrote, but
I have decided what I must do, and there isn't
going to be any turning back. It is very sweet
and generous and dear of you to wish to send
me to Europe this summer--for the moment I
was intoxicated by the idea; but sober second
thoughts said no. It would be rather illogical
of me to refuse to take your money for college,
and then use it instead just for amusement! You
mustn't get me used to too many luxuries. One
doesn't miss what one has never had; but it's
awfully hard going without things after one has

commenced thinking they are his--hers (English language needs another pronoun) by natural right. Living with Sallie and Julia is an awful strain on my stoical philosophy. They have both had things from the time they were babies; they accept happiness as a matter of course. The World, they think, owes them everything they want. Maybe the World does--in any case, it seems to acknowledge the debt and pay up. But as for me, it owes me nothing, and distinctly told me so in the beginning. I have no right to borrow on credit, for there will come a time when the World will repudiate my claim.

I seem to be floundering in a sea of metaphor--but I hope you grasp my meaning? Anyway, I have a very strong feeling that the only honest thing for me to do is to teach this summer and begin to support myself.

MAGNOLIA,

Four days later

I'd got just that much written, when--what do you think happened? The maid arrived with Master Jervie's card. He is going abroad too this summer; not with Julia and her family, but entirely by himself I told him that you had invited me to go with a lady who is chaperoning a party of girls. He knows about you, Daddy. That is, he knows that my father and mother are dead, and that a kind gentleman is sending me to college; I simply didn't have the courage to tell him about the John Grier Home and all the rest. He thinks that you are my guardian and a perfectly legitimate old family friend. I have never told him that I didn't know you--that would seem too queer!

Anyway, he insisted on my going to Europe. He said that it was a necessary part of my education and that I mustn't think of refusing. Also, that he would be in Paris at the same time, and that we would run away from the chaperon occasionally and have dinner together at nice, funny, foreign restaurants.

Well, Daddy, it did appeal to me! I almost weakened; if he hadn't been so dictatorial, maybe I should have entirely weakened. I can be enticed step by step, but I WON't be forced. He said I was a silly, foolish, irrational, quixotic, idiotic, stubborn child (those are a few of his abusive adjectives; the rest escape me), and that I didn't know what was good for me; I ought to let older people judge. We almost quarrelled--I am not sure but that we entirely did!

In any case, I packed my trunk fast and came up here. I thought I'd better see my bridges in flames behind me before I finished writing to you. They are entirely reduced to ashes now. Here I am at Cliff Top (the name of Mrs. Paterson's cottage) with my trunk unpacked and Florence (the little one) already struggling with first declension nouns. And it bids fair to be a struggle! She is a most uncommonly spoiled child; I shall have to teach her first how to study--she has never in her life concentrated on anything more difficult than ice-cream soda water.

We use a quiet corner of the cliffs for a schoolroom--Mrs. Paterson wishes me to keep them out of doors--and I will say that I find it difficult to concentrate with the blue sea before me and ships a-sailing by! And when I think I might be on one, sailing off to foreign lands--but I WON't let myself think of anything but Latin Grammar.

The prepositions a or ab, absque, coram, cum, de e or ex, prae, pro, sine, tenus, in, subter, sub and super govern the ablative.

So you see, Daddy, I am already plunged into work with my eyes persistently set against temptation. Don't be cross with me, please, and don't think that I do not appreciate your kindness, for I do--always--always. The only way I can ever repay you is by turning out a Very Useful Citizen (Are women citizens? I don't suppose they are.) Anyway, a Very Useful Person. And when you look at me you can say, 'I gave that Very Useful Person to the world.'

That sounds well, doesn't it, Daddy? But I don't wish to mislead you. The feeling often comes over me that I am not at all remarkable; it is fun to plan a career, but in all probability I shan't turn out a bit different from any other ordinary person. I may end by marrying an undertaker and being an inspiration to him in his work.

Yours ever,
Judy

19th August

Dear Daddy-Long-Legs,

My window looks out on the loveliest landscape--ocean-scape, rather--nothing but water and rocks.

The summer goes. I spend the morning with Latin and English and algebra and my two stupid girls. I don't know how Marion is ever going to get into college, or stay in after she gets there. And as for Florence, she is hopeless--but oh! such a little beauty. I don't suppose it matters in the least whether they are stupid or not so long as they are pretty? One can't help thinking, though, how their conversation will bore their husbands, unless they are fortunate enough to obtain stupid husbands. I suppose that's quite possible; the world seems to be filled with stupid men; I've met a number this summer.

In the afternoon we take a walk on the cliffs, or swim, if the tide is right. I can swim in salt water with the utmost ease you see my education is already being put to use!

A letter comes from Mr. Jervis Pendleton in Paris, rather a short concise letter; I'm not quite forgiven yet for refusing to follow his advice. However, if he gets back in time, he will see me for a few days at Lock Willow before college opens, and if I am very nice and sweet and docile, I shall (I am led to infer) be received into favour again.

Also a letter from Sallie. She wants me to come to their camp for two weeks in September. Must I ask your permission, or haven't I yet arrived at the place where I can do as I please? Yes, I am sure I have--I'm a Senior, you know. Having worked all summer, I feel like taking a little healthful recreation; I want to see the Adirondacks; I want to see Sallie; I want to see Sallie's brother--he's going to teach me to canoe--and (we come to my chief motive, which is mean) I want Master Jervie to arrive at Lock Willow and find me not there.

I MUST show him that he can't dictate to me. No one can dictate to me but you, Daddy--and you can't always! I'm off for the woods.

Judy

CAMP MCBRIDE,

6th September

Dear Daddy,

Your letter didn't come in time (I am pleased to say). If you wish your instructions to be obeyed, you must have your secretary transmit them in less than two weeks. As you observe, I am here, and have been for five days.

The woods are fine, and so is the camp, and so is the weather, and so are the McBrides, and so is the whole world. I'm very happy!

There's Jimmie calling for me to come canoeing. Goodbye--sorry to have disobeyed, but why are you so persistent about not wanting me to play a little? When I've worked all the summer I deserve two weeks. You are awfully dog-in-the-mangerish.

However--I love you still, Daddy, in spite of all your faults.

Judy

3rd October

Dear Daddy- Long- Legs,

Back at college and a Senior--also editor of the Monthly. It doesn't seem possible, does it, that so sophisticated a person, just four years ago, was an inmate of the John Grier Home? We do arrive fast in America!

What do you think of this? A note from Master Jervie directed to Lock Willow and forwarded here. He's sorry, but he finds that he can't get up there this autumn; he has accepted an invitation to go yachting with some friends. Hopes I've had a nice summer and am enjoying the country.

And he knew all the time that I was with the McBrides, for Julia told him so! You men ought to leave intrigue to women; you haven't a light enough touch.

Julia has a trunkful of the most ravishing new clothes--an evening gown of rainbow Liberty crepe that would be fitting raiment for the angels in Paradise. And I thought that my own clothes this year were unprecedentedly (is there such a word?) beautiful. I copied Mrs. Paterson's wardrobe with the aid of a cheap dressmaker, and though the gowns didn't turn out quite twins of the originals, I was entirely happy until Julia unpacked. But now--I live to see Paris!

Dear Daddy, aren't you glad you're not a girl? I suppose you think that the fuss we make over clothes is too absolutely silly? It is. No doubt about it. But it's entirely your fault.

Did you ever hear about the learned Herr Professor who regarded unnecessary adornment with contempt and favoured sensible, utilitarian clothes for women? His wife, who was an obliging creature, adopted 'dress reform.' And what do you think he did? He eloped with a chorus girl.

Yours ever,

Judy

PS. The chamber-maid in our corridor wears blue checked gingham aprons. I am going to get her some brown ones instead, and sink the blue ones in the bottom of the lake. I have a reminiscent chill every time I look at them.

17th November

Dear Daddy-Long-Legs,

Such a blight has fallen over my literary career. I don't know whether to tell you or not, but I would like some sympathy--silent sympathy, please; don't re-open the wound by referring to it in your next letter.

I've been writing a book, all last winter in the evenings, and all the summer when I wasn't teaching Latin to my two stupid children. I just finished it before college opened and sent it to a publisher. He kept it two months, and I was certain he was going to take it; but yesterday morning an express parcel came (thirty cents due) and there it was back again with a letter from the publisher, a very nice, fatherly letter-- but frank! He said he saw from the address that I was still at college, and if I would accept some advice, he would suggest that I put all of my energy into my lessons and wait until I graduated before beginning to write. He enclosed his reader's opinion. Here it is:

'Plot highly improbable. Characterization exaggerated. Conversation unnatural. A good deal of humour but not always in the best of taste. Tell her to keep on trying, and in time she may produce a real book.'

Not on the whole flattering, is it, Daddy? And I thought I was making a notable addition to American literature. I did truly. I was planning to surprise you by writing a great novel before I graduated. I collected the material for it while I was at Julia's last Christmas. But I dare say the editor is right. Probably two weeks was not enough in which to observe the manners and customs of a great city.

I took it walking with me yesterday afternoon, and when I came to the gas house, I went in and asked the engineer if I might borrow his furnace. He politely opened the door, and with my own hands I chucked it in. I felt as though I had cremated my only child!

I went to bed last night utterly dejected; I thought I was never going to amount to anything, and that you had thrown away your money for nothing. But what do you think? I woke up this morning with a beautiful new plot in my head, and I've been going about all day planning my characters, just as happy as I could be. No one can ever accuse me of being a pessimist! If I had a husband and twelve children swallowed by an earthquake one day, I'd bob up smilingly the next morning and commence to look for another set.

Affectionately,

Judy

14th December

Dear Daddy-Long-Legs,

I dreamed the funniest dream last night. I

thought I went into a book store and the clerk brought me a new book named The Life and Letters of Judy Abbott. I could see it perfectly plainly--red cloth binding with a picture of the John Grier Home on the cover, and my portrait for a frontispiece with, 'very truly yours, Judy Abbott,' written below. But just as I was turning to the end to read the inscription on my tombstone, I woke up. It was very annoying! I almost found out whom I'm going to marry and when I'm going to die.

Don't you think it would be interesting if you really could read the story of your life--written perfectly truthfully by an omniscient author? And suppose you could only read it on this condition: that you would never forget it, but would have to go through life knowing ahead of time exactly how everything you did would turn out, and foreseeing to the exact hour the time when you would die. How many people do you suppose would have the courage to read it then?

or how many could suppress their curiosity sufficiently to escape from reading it, even at the price of having to live without hope and without surprises?

Life is monotonous enough at best; you have to eat and sleep about so often. But imagine how DEADLY monotonous it would be if nothing unexpected could happen between meals. Mercy! Daddy, there's a blot, but I'm on the third page and I can't begin a new sheet.

I'm going on with biology again this year--very interesting subject; we're studying the alimentary system at present. You should see how sweet a cross-section of the duodenum of a cat is under the microscope.

Also we've arrived at philosophy--interesting but evanescent. I prefer biology where you can pin the subject under discussion to a board. There's another! And another! This pen is weeping copiously. Please excuse its tears.

Do you believe in free will? I do--unreservedly. I don't agree at all with the philosophers who think that every action is the absolutely inevitable and automatic resultant of an aggregation of remote causes. That's the most immoral doctrine I ever heard--nobody would be to blame for anything. If a man believed in fatalism, he would naturally just sit down and say, 'the Lord's will be done,' and continue to sit until he fell over dead.

I believe absolutely in my own free will and my own power to accomplish--and that is the belief that moves mountains. You watch me become a great author! I have four chapters of my new book finished and five more drafted.

This is a very abstruse letter--does your head ache, Daddy? I think we'll stop now and make some fudge. I'm sorry I can't send you a piece; it will be unusually good, for we're going to make it with real cream and three butter balls.

Yours affectionately,

Judy

PS. We're having fancy dancing in gymnasium class. You can see by the accompanying picture how much we look like a real ballet. The one at the end accomplishing a graceful pirouette is me--I mean I.

26th December

My Dear, Dear, Daddy,

Haven't you any sense? Don't you KNOW that you mustn't give one girl seventeen Christmas presents? I'm a Socialist, please remember; do you wish to turn me into a Plutocrat?

Think how embarrassing it would be if we should ever quarrel! I should have to engage a moving-van to return your gifts.

I am sorry that the necktie I sent was so wobbly; I knit it with my own hands (as you doubtless discovered from internal evidence). You will have to wear it on cold days and keep your coat buttoned up tight.

Thank you, Daddy, a thousand times. I think

you're the sweetest man that ever lived--and the foolishest!

Judy

PS. Here's a four-leaf clover from Camp McBride to bring you good luck for the New Year.

9th January

Do you wish to do something, Daddy, that will ensure your eternal salvation? There is a family here who are in awfully desperate straits. A mother and father and four visible children--the two older boys have disappeared into the world to make their fortune and have not sent any of it back. The father worked in a glass

factory and got consumption--it's awfully un-
healthy work--and now has been sent away
to a hospital. That took all their savings, and
the support of the family falls upon the oldest
daughter, who is twenty-four. She dressmakes
for $1.50 a day (when she can get it) and em-
broiders centrepieces in the evening. The mother isn't very strong and is extremely ineffectual
and pious. She sits with her hands folded, a picture of patient resignation, while the daughter
kills herself with overwork and responsibility
and worry; she doesn't see how they are going
to get through the rest of the winter--and I don't
either. One hundred dollars would buy some
coal and some shoes for three children so that
they could go to school, and give a little margin
so that she needn't worry herself to death when
a few days pass and she doesn't get work.

You are the richest man I know. Don't you
suppose you could spare one hundred dollars?
That girl deserves help a lot more than I ever

did. I wouldn't ask it except for the girl; I don't care much what happens to the mother--she is such a jelly-fish.

The way people are for ever rolling their eyes to heaven and saying, 'Perhaps it's all for the best,' when they are perfectly dead sure it's not, makes me enraged. Humility or resignation or whatever you choose to call it, is simply impotent inertia. I'm for a more militant religion!

We are getting the most dreadful lessons in philosophy--all of Schopenhauer for tomorrow. The professor doesn't seem to realize that we are taking any other subject. He's a queer old duck; he goes about with his head in the clouds and blinks dazedly when occasionally he strikes solid earth. He tries to lighten his lectures with an occasional witticism--and we do our best to smile, but I assure you his jokes are no laughing matter. He spends his entire time between classes in trying to figure out whether matter really exists or whether he only thinks it exists.

I'm sure my sewing girl hasn't any doubt but that it exists!

Where do you think my new novel is? In the waste-basket. I can see myself that it's no good on earth, and when a loving author realizes that, what WOULD be the judgment of a critical public?

Later

I address you, Daddy, from a bed of pain. For two days I've been laid up with swollen tonsils; I can just swallow hot milk, and that is all. 'What were your parents thinking of not to have those tonsils out when you were a baby?' the doctor wished to know. I'm sure I haven't an idea, but I doubt if they were thinking much about me.

Yours,

J. A.

Next morning

I just read this over before sealing it. I don't know WHY I cast such a misty atmosphere over life. I hasten to assure you that I am young and happy and exuberant; and I trust you are the same. Youth has nothing to do with birthdays, only with ALIVEDNESS of spirit, so even if your hair is grey, Daddy, you can still be a boy.

Affectionately,

Judy

12th Jan.

Dear Mr. Philanthropist,

Your cheque for my family came yesterday. Thank you so much! I cut gymnasium and took it down to them right after luncheon, and you should have seen the girl's face! She was so surprised and happy and relieved that she looked almost young; and she's only twenty-four. Isn't it pitiful?

Anyway, she feels now as though all the good things were coming together. She has steady work ahead for two months--someone's getting married, and there's a trousseau to make.

'thank the good Lord!' cried the mother, when she grasped the fact that that small piece of paper was one hundred dollars.

'It wasn't the good Lord at all,' said I, 'it was Daddy-Long-Legs.' (Mr. Smith, I called you.)

'But it was the good Lord who put it in his mind,' said she.

'Not at all! I put it in his mind myself,' said I.

But anyway, Daddy, I trust the good Lord will reward you suitably. You deserve ten thousand years out of purgatory.

Yours most gratefully,

Judy Abbott

15th Feb.

May it please Your Most Excellent Majesty: This morning I did eat my breakfast upon a cold turkey pie and a goose, and I did send for a cup of tee (a china drink) of which I had never drank before.

Don't be nervous, Daddy--I haven't lost my mind; I'm merely quoting Sam'l Pepys. We're reading him in connection with English History, original sources. Sallie and Julia and I converse now in the language of 1660. Listen to this:

'I went to Charing Cross to see Major Harrison hanged, drawn and quartered: he looking as cheerful as any man could do in that condition.' And this: 'dined with my lady who is in handsome mourning for her brother who died yesterday of spotted fever.'

Seems a little early to commence entertaining, doesn't it? A friend of Pepys devised a very cunning manner whereby the king might pay his debts out of the sale to poor people of old decayed provisions. What do you, a reformer, think of that? I don't believe we're so bad today as the newspapers make out.

Samuel was as excited about his clothes as any girl; he spent five times as much on dress as his wife--that appears to have been the Golden Age of husbands. Isn't this a touching entry? You see he really was honest. 'today came home my fine Camlett cloak with gold buttons, which cost me much money, and I pray God to make me able to pay for it.'

Excuse me for being so full of Pepys; I'm writing a special topic on him.

What do you think, Daddy? The Self-Government Association has abolished the ten o'clock rule. We can keep our lights all night if we choose, the only requirement being that we do not disturb others--we are not supposed to entertain on a large scale. The result is a beautiful commentary on human nature. Now that we may stay up as long as we choose, we no longer choose. Our heads begin to nod at nine o'clock, and by nine-thirty the pen drops from our nerveless grasp. It's nine-thirty now. Good night.

Sunday

Just back from church--preacher from Georgia. We must take care, he says, not to develop our intellects at the expense of our emotional natures--but methought it was a poor, dry sermon (Pepys again). It doesn't matter what part of the United States or Canada they come from, or what denomination they are, we always get the same sermon. Why on earth don't they go to men's colleges and urge the students not to allow their manly natures to be crushed out by too much mental application?

It's a beautiful day--frozen and icy and clear. As soon as dinner is over, Sallie and Julia and Marty Keene and Eleanor Pratt (friends of mine, but you don't know them) and I are going to put on short skirts and walk 'cross country to Crystal Spring Farm and have a fried chicken and waffle supper, and then have Mr. Crystal Spring drive us home in his buckboard. We are supposed to be inside the campus at seven, but we are going to stretch a point tonight and make it eight.

Farewell, kind Sir.

I have the honour of subscribing myself,
Your most loyall, dutifull, faithfull and obedient servant,

J. Abbott

March Fifth

Dear Mr. Trustee,

Tomorrow is the first Wednesday in the month--a weary day for the John Grier Home. How relieved they'll be when five o'clock comes and you pat them on the head and take yourselves off! Did you (individually) ever pat me on the head, Daddy? I don't believe so--my memory seems to be concerned only with fat Trustees.

Give the Home my love, please--my TRULY love. I have quite a feeling of tenderness for it as I look back through a haze of four years. When I first came to college I felt quite resentful because

I'd been robbed of the normal kind of childhood that the other girls had had; but now, I don't feel that way in the least. I regard it as a very unusual adventure. It gives me a sort of vantage point from which to stand aside and look at life. Emerging full grown, I get a perspective on the world, that other people who have been brought up in the thick of things entirely lack.

I know lots of girls (Julia, for instance) who never know that they are happy. They are so accustomed to the feeling that their senses are deadened to it; but as for me--I am perfectly sure every moment of my life that I am happy. And I'm going to keep on being, no matter what unpleasant things turn up. I'm going to regard them (even toothaches) as interesting experiences, and be glad to know what they feel like. 'Whatever sky's above me, I've a heart for any fate.'

However, Daddy, don't take this new affection for the J.G.H. too literally. If I have five children, like Rousseau, I shan't leave them on the steps of a foundling asylum in order to insure their being brought up simply.

Give my kindest regards to Mrs. Lippett (that, I think, is truthful; love would be a little strong) and don't forget to tell her what a beautiful nature I've developed.

Affectionately,

Judy

LOCK WILLOW,

4th April

Dear Daddy,

Do you observe the postmark? Sallie and I are embellishing Lock Willow with our presence during the Easter Vacation. We decided that the best thing we could do with our ten days was to come where it is quiet. Our nerves had got to the point where they wouldn't stand another meal in Fergussen. Dining in a room with four hundred girls is an ordeal when you are tired. There is so much noise that you can't hear the girls across the table speak unless they make their hands into a megaphone and shout. That is the truth.

We are tramping over the hills and reading and writing, and having a nice, restful time. We climbed to the top of 'sky Hill' this morning where Master Jervie and I once cooked supper--it doesn't seem possible that it was nearly two years ago. I could still see the place where the smoke of our fire blackened the rock. It is funny how certain places get connected with certain people, and you never go back without thinking of them. I was quite lonely without him--for two minutes.

What do you think is my latest activity, Daddy? You will begin to believe that I am incorrigible--I am writing a book. I started it three weeks ago and am eating it up in chunks. I've caught the secret. Master Jervie and that editor man were right; you are most convincing when you write about the things you know. And this time it is about something that I do know--exhaustively. Guess where it's laid? In the John Grier Home! And it's good, Daddy, I actually believe it is--just about the tiny little things that happened every day. I'm a realist now. I've abandoned romanticism; I shall go back to it later though, when my own adventurous future begins.

This new book is going to get itself finished--and published! You see if it doesn't. If you just want a thing hard enough and keep on trying, you do get it in the end. I've been trying for four years to get a letter from you--and I haven't given up hope yet.

Goodbye, Daddy dear,

(I like to call you Daddy dear; it's so alliterative.)

Affectionately,

Judy

PS. I forgot to tell you the farm news, but it's very distressing. Skip this postscript if you don't want your sensibilities all wrought up.

Poor old Grove is dead. He got so that he couldn't chew and they had to shoot him.

Nine chickens were killed by a weasel or a skunk or a rat last week.

One of the cows is sick, and we had to have the veterinary surgeon out from Bonnyrigg Four Corners. Amasai stayed up all night to give her linseed oil and whisky. But we have an awful suspicion that the poor sick cow got nothing but linseed oil.

Sentimental Tommy (the tortoise-shell cat) has disappeared; we are afraid he has been caught in a trap.

There are lots of troubles in the world!

17th May

Dear Daddy-Long-Legs,

This is going to be extremely short because my shoulder aches at the sight of a pen. Lecture notes all day, immortal novel all evening, make too much writing.

Commencement three weeks from next Wednesday. I think you might come and make my acquaintance--I shall hate you if you don't! Julia's inviting Master Jervie, he being her family, and Sallie's inviting Jimmie McB., he being her family, but who is there for me to invite? Just you and Lippett, and I don't want her. Please come.

Yours, with love and writer's cramp.

Judy

LOCK WILLOW,

19th June

Dear Daddy-Long-Legs,

I'm educated! My diploma is in the bottom bureau drawer with my two best dresses. Commencement was as usual, with a few showers at vital moments. Thank you for your rosebuds. They were lovely. Master Jervie and Master Jimmie both gave me roses, too, but I left theirs in the bath tub and carried yours in the class procession.

Here I am at Lock Willow for the summer--for ever maybe. The board is cheap; the surroundings quiet and conducive to a literary life. What more does a struggling author wish? I am mad about my book. I think of it every waking moment, and dream of it at night. All I want is peace and quiet and lots of time to work (interspersed with nourishing meals).

Master Jervie is coming up for a week or so in August, and Jimmie McBride is going to drop in sometime through the summer. He's connected with a bond house now, and goes about the country selling bonds to banks. He's going to combine the 'Farmers' National' at the Corners and me on the same trip.

You see that Lock Willow isn't entirely lacking in society. I'd be expecting to have you come motoring through--only I know now that that is hopeless. When you wouldn't come to my commencement, I tore you from my heart and buried you for ever.

Judy Abbott, A.B.

24th July

Dearest Daddy-Long-Legs,

Isn't it fun to work--or don't you ever do it? It's especially fun when your kind of work is the thing you'd rather do more than anything else in the world. I've been writing as fast as my pen would go every day this summer, and my only quarrel with life is that the days aren't long enough to write all the beautiful and valuable and entertaining thoughts I'm thinking.

I've finished the second draft of my book and am going to begin the third tomorrow morning at half-past seven. It's the sweetest book you ever saw--it is, truly. I think of nothing else. I can barely wait in the morning to dress and eat before beginning; then I write and write and write till suddenly I'm so tired that I'm limp all over. Then I go out with Colin (the new sheep dog) and romp through the fields and get a fresh supply of ideas for the next day. It's the most beautiful book you ever saw--Oh, pardon--I said that before.

You don't think me conceited, do you, Daddy dear?

I'm not, really, only just now I'm in the enthusiastic stage. Maybe later on I'll get cold and critical and sniffy. No, I'm sure I won't! This time I've written a real book. Just wait till you see it.

I'll try for a minute to talk about something else. I never told you, did I, that Amasai and Carrie got married last May? They are still working here, but so far as I can see it has spoiled them both. She used to laugh when he tramped in mud or dropped ashes on the floor, but now--you should hear her scold! And she doesn't curl her hair any longer. Amasai, who used to be so obliging about beating rugs and carrying wood, grumbles if you suggest such a thing. Also his neckties are quite dingy--black and brown, where they used to be scarlet and purple. I've determined never to marry. It's a deteriorating process, evidently.

There isn't much of any farm news. The animals are all in the best of health. The pigs are unusually fat, the cows seem contented and the hens are laying well. Are you interested in poultry? If so, let me recommend that invaluable little work, 200 Eggs per Hen per Year. I am thinking of starting an incubator next spring and raising broilers. You see I'm settled at Lock Willow permanently. I have decided to stay until I've written 114 novels like Anthony Trollope's mother. Then I shall have completed my life work and can retire and travel.

Mr. James McBride spent last Sunday with us. Fried chicken and ice-cream for dinner, both of which he appeared to appreciate. I was awfully glad to see him; he brought a momentary reminder that the world at large exists. Poor Jimmie is having a hard time peddling his bonds. The 'Farmers' National' at the Corners wouldn't have anything to do with them in spite of the fact that they pay six per cent. interest and sometimes seven. I think he'll end up by going home to Worcester and taking a job in his father's factory. He's too open and confiding and kind-hearted ever to make a successful financier. But to be the manager of a flourishing overall factory is a very desirable position, don't you think? Just now he turns up his nose at overalls, but he'll come to them.

I hope you appreciate the fact that this is a long letter from a person with writer's cramp. But I still love you, Daddy dear, and I'm very happy. With beautiful scenery all about, and lots to eat and a comfortable four-post bed and a ream of blank paper and a pint of ink--what more does one want in the world?

Yours as always,

Judy

PS. The postman arrives with some more news. We are to expect Master Jervie on Friday next to spend a week. That's a very pleasant prospect--only I am afraid my poor book will suffer. Master Jervie is very demanding.

27th August

Dear Daddy-Long-Legs,

Where are you, I wonder?

I never know what part of the world you are in, but I hope you're not in New York during this awful weather. I hope you're on a mountain peak (but not in Switzerland; somewhere nearer) looking at the snow and thinking about me. Please be thinking about me. I'm quite lonely and I want to be thought about. Oh, Daddy, I wish I knew you! Then when we were unhappy we could cheer each other up.

I don't think I can stand much more of Lock Willow. I'm thinking of moving. Sallie is going to do settlement work in Boston next winter. Don't you think it would be nice for me to go with her, then we could have a studio together? I would write while she SETTLED and we could be together in the evenings. Evenings are very long when there's no one but the Semples and Carrie and Amasai to talk to. I know in advance that you won't like my studio idea. I can read your secretary's letter now:

"Miss Jerusha Abbott.

"DEAR MADAM,

"Mr. Smith prefers that you remain at Lock Willow.

'Yours truly,

"*ELMER H. GRIGGS.*"

I hate your secretary. I am certain that a man named Elmer H. Griggs must be horrid. But truly, Daddy, I think I shall have to go to Boston. I can't stay here. If something doesn't happen soon, I shall throw myself into the silo pit out of sheer desperation.

Mercy! but it's hot. All the grass is burnt up and the brooks are dry and the roads are dusty. It hasn't rained for weeks and weeks.

This letter sounds as though I had hydrophobia, but I haven't. I just want some family.

Goodbye, my dearest Daddy.

I wish I knew you.

Judy

LOCK WILLOW,

19th September

Dear Daddy,

Something has happened and I need advice. I need it from you, and from nobody else in the world. Wouldn't it be possible for me to see you? It's so much easier to talk than to write; and I'm afraid your secretary might open the letter. Judy

PS. I'm very unhappy.

LOCK WILLOW,

3rd October

Dear Daddy-Long-Legs,

Your note written in your own hand--and a pretty wobbly hand!--came this morning. I am so sorry that you have been ill; I wouldn't have bothered you with my affairs if I had known. Yes, I will tell you the trouble, but it's sort of complicated to write, and VERY PRIVATE. Please don't keep this letter, but burn it.

Before I begin--here's a cheque for one thousand dollars. It seems funny, doesn't it, for me to be sending a cheque to you? Where do you think I got it?

I've sold my story, Daddy. It's going to be published serially in seven parts, and then in a book! You might think I'd be wild with joy, but I'm not. I'm entirely apathetic. Of course I'm glad to begin paying you--I owe you over two thousand more. It's coming in instalments. Now don't be horrid, please, about taking it, because it makes me happy to return it. I owe you a great deal more than the mere money, and the rest I will continue to pay all my life in gratitude and affection.

And now, Daddy, about the other thing; please give me your most worldly advice, whether you think I'll like it or not.

You know that I've always had a very special feeling towards you; you sort of represented my whole family; but you won't mind, will you, if I tell you that I have a very much more special feeling for another man? You can probably guess without much trouble who he is. I suspect that my letters have been very full of Master Jervie for a very long time.

I wish I could make you understand what he is like and how entirely companionable we are. We think the same about everything--I am afraid I have a tendency to make over my ideas to match his! But he is almost always right; he ought to be, you know, for he has fourteen years' start of me. In other ways, though, he's just an overgrown boy, and he does need looking after--he hasn't any sense about wearing rubbers when it rains. He and I always think the same things are funny, and that is such a lot; it's dreadful when two people's senses of humour are antagonistic. I don't believe there's any bridging that gulf!

And he is--Oh, well! He is just himself, and I miss him, and miss him, and miss him. The whole world seems empty and aching. I hate the moonlight because it's beautiful and he isn't here to see it with me. But maybe you've loved somebody, too, and you know? If you have, I don't need to explain; if you haven't, I can't explain.

Anyway, that's the way I feel--and I've refused to marry him.

I didn't tell him why; I was just dumb and miserable. I couldn't think of anything to say. And now he has gone away imagining that I want to marry Jimmie McBride--I don't in the least, I wouldn't think of marrying Jimmie; he isn't grown up enough. But Master Jervie and I got into a dreadful muddle of misunderstanding and we both hurt each other's feelings. The reason I sent him away was not because I didn't care for him, but because I cared for him so much. I was afraid he would regret it in the future--and I couldn't stand that! It didn't seem right for a person of my lack of antecedents to marry into any such family as his. I never told him about the orphan asylum, and I hated to explain that I didn't know who I was. I may be DREADFUL, you know. And his family are proud--and I'm proud, too!

Also, I felt sort of bound to you. After having been educated to be a writer, I must at least try to be one; it would scarcely be fair to accept your education and then go off and not use it. But now that I am going to be able to pay back the money, I feel that I have partially discharged that debt--besides, I suppose I could keep on being a writer even if I did marry. The two professions are not necessarily exclusive.

I've been thinking very hard about it. Of course he is a Socialist, and he has unconventional ideas; maybe he wouldn't mind marrying into the proletariat so much as some men might. Perhaps when two people are exactly in accord, and always happy when together and lonely when apart, they ought not to let anything in the world stand between them. Of course I WANT to believe that! But I'd like to get your unemotional opinion. You probably belong to a Family also, and will look at it from a worldly point of view and not just a sympathetic, human point of view--so you see how brave I am to lay it before you.

Suppose I go to him and explain that the trouble isn't Jimmie, but is the John Grier Home--would that be a dreadful thing for me to do? It would take a great deal of courage. I'd almost rather be miserable for the rest of my life.

This happened nearly two months ago; I haven't heard a word from him since he was here. I was just getting sort of acclimated to the feeling of a broken heart, when a letter came from Julia that stirred me all up again. She said--very casually--that 'Uncle Jervis' had been caught out all night in a storm when he was hunting in Canada, and had been ill ever since with pneumonia. And I never knew it. I was feeling hurt because he had just disappeared into blankness without a word. I think he's pretty unhappy, and I know I am!

What seems to you the right thing for me to do?

Judy

6th October

Dearest Daddy-Long-Legs,

Yes, certainly I'll come--at half-past four next Wednesday afternoon. Of COURSE I can find the way. I've been in New York three times and am not quite a baby. I can't believe that I am really going to see you--I've been just THINKING you so long that it hardly seems as though you are a tangible flesh-and-blood person.

You are awfully good, Daddy, to bother yourself with me, when you're not strong. Take care and don't catch cold. These fall rains are very damp.

Affectionately,

Judy

PS. I've just had an awful thought. Have you a butler? I'm afraid of butlers, and if one opens the door I shall faint upon the step. What can I say to him? You didn't tell me your name. Shall I ask for Mr. Smith?

Thursday Morning

My Very Dearest Master-Jervie-Daddy-Long-Legs Pendleton-Smith,

Did you sleep last night? I didn't. Not a

single wink. I was too amazed and excited and bewildered and happy. I don't believe I ever shall sleep again--or eat either. But I hope you slept; you must, you know, because then you will get well faster and can come to me.

Dear Man, I can't bear to think how ill you've been--and all the time I never knew it. When the doctor came down yesterday to put me in the cab, he told me that for three days they gave you up. Oh, dearest, if that had happened, the light would have gone out of the world for me. I suppose that some day in the far future--one of us must leave the other; but at least we shall have had our happiness and there will be memories to live with.

I meant to cheer you up--and instead I have to cheer myself. For in spite of being happier than I ever dreamed I could be, I'm also soberer. The fear that something may happen rests like a shadow on my heart. Always before I could be frivolous and care-free and unconcerned, because I had nothing precious to lose. But now--I shall have a Great Big Worry all the rest of my life. Whenever you are away from me I shall be thinking of all the automobiles that can run over you, or the sign-boards that can fall on your head, or the dreadful, squirmy germs that you may be swallowing. My peace of mind is gone for ever--but anyway, I never cared much for just plain peace.

Please get well--fast--fast--fast. I want to have you close by where I can touch you and make sure you are tangible. Such a little half hour we had together! I'm afraid maybe I dreamed it. If I were only a member of your family (a very distant fourth cousin) then I could come and visit you every day, and read aloud and plump up your pillow and smooth out those two little wrinkles in your forehead and make the corners of your mouth turn up in a nice cheerful smile. But you are cheerful again, aren't you? You were yesterday before I left. The doctor said I must be a good nurse, that you looked ten years younger. I hope that being in love doesn't make every one ten years younger. Will you still care for me, darling, if I turn out to be only eleven?

Yesterday was the most wonderful day that could ever happen. If I live to be ninety-nine I shall never forget the tiniest detail. The girl that left Lock Willow at dawn was a very different person from the one who came back at night. Mrs. Semple called me at half-past four. I started wide awake in the darkness and the first thought that popped into my head was, 'I am going to see Daddy-Long-Legs!' I ate breakfast in the kitchen by candle-light, and then drove the five miles to the station through the most glorious October colouring. The sun came up on the way, and the swamp maples and dogwood glowed crimson and orange and the stone walls and cornfields sparkled with hoar frost; the air was keen and clear and full of promise. I knew something was going to happen. All the way in the train the rails kept singing, 'You're going to see Daddy-Long-Legs.' It made me feel secure. I had such faith in Daddy's ability to set things right. And I knew that somewhere another man--dearer than Daddy--was wanting to see me, and somehow I had a feeling that before the journey ended I should meet him, too. And you see!

When I came to the house on Madison Avenue it looked so big and brown and forbidding that I didn't dare go in, so I walked around the block to get up my courage. But I needn't have been a bit afraid; your butler is such a nice, fatherly old man that he made me feel at home at once. 'Is this Miss Abbott?' he said to me, and I said, 'Yes,' so I didn't have to ask for Mr. Smith after all. He told me to wait in the drawing-room. It was a very sombre, magnificent, man's sort of room. I sat down on the edge of a big upholstered chair and kept saying to myself:

'I'm going to see Daddy-Long-Legs! I'm going to see Daddy-Long-Legs!'

Then presently the man came back and asked me please to step up to the library. I was so excited that really and truly my feet would hardly take me up. Outside the door he turned and whispered, 'He's been very ill, Miss. This is the first day he's been allowed to sit up. You'll not stay long enough to excite him?' I knew from the way he said it that he loved you--an I think he's an old dear!

Then he knocked and said, 'miss Abbott,' and I went in and the door closed behind me.

It was so dim coming in from the brightly lighted hall that for a moment I could scarcely make out anything; then I saw a big easy chair before the fire and a shining tea table with a smaller chair beside it. And I realized that a man was sitting in the big chair propped up by pillows with a rug over his knees. Before I could stop him he rose--rather shakily--and steadied himself by the back of the chair and just looked at me without a word. And then--and then--I saw it was you! But even with that I didn't understand. I thought Daddy had had you come there to meet me or a surprise.

Then you laughed and held out your hand and said, 'dear little Judy, couldn't you guess that I was Daddy-Long-Legs?'

In an instant it flashed over me. Oh, but I have been stupid! A hundred little things might have told me, if I had had any wits. I wouldn't make a very good detective, would I, Daddy? Jervie? What must I call you? Just plain Jervie sounds disrespectful, and I can't be disrespectful to you!

It was a very sweet half hour before your doctor came and sent me away. I was so dazed when I got to the station that I almost took a train for St Louis. And you were pretty dazed, too. You forgot to give me any tea. But we're both very, very happy, aren't we? I drove back to Lock Willow in the dark but oh, how the stars were shining! And this morning I've been out with Colin visiting all the places that you and I went to together, and remembering what you said and how you looked. The woods today are burnished bronze and the air is full of frost. It's CLIMBING weather. I wish you were here to climb the hills with me. I am missing you dreadfully, Jervie dear, but it's a happy kind of missing; we'll be together soon. We belong to each other now really and truly, no make-believe. Doesn't it seem queer for me to belong to someone at last? It seems very, very sweet.

And I shall never let you be sorry for a single instant.

Yours, for ever and ever,
Judy

PS. This is the first love-letter I ever wrote. Isn't it funny that I know how?

END

나만의 리뷰 and 명문장